Landmark
BOOKS

EXPLORING
THE
HIMALAYA

EXPLORING
THE
HIMĀLĀYA

WILLIAM O. DOUGLAS

Illustrations by Clarence Doore

RANDOM HOUSE : NEW YORK

To my stepdaughter, Joan Davidson,
and my niece, Mary Douglas,
who read the first draft
and improved it immeasurably.

Contents

FOREWORD

A traveler from the West who these days visits the Himalaya is likely first to see them from the air. But whether he comes by plane, rail, auto, or on foot, he finds a massive barricade of snow and ice stretching for miles. Clusters of white peaks rise above broken ranges; single peaks stand in isolated splendor; sheets of ice run for dozens of miles on end.

One naturally assumes that these peaks overlook

wild and desolate valleys, that this region is barred to man except for the skilled alpinist. But that assumption is false. People live here. They herd their sheep up to 18,000 feet in the summer months. Their yaks range the high 15,000 foot basins and graze to 20,000 feet. Villages are found as high as 13,000 feet; barley and hay are grown there. Here people hole up in stone huts for the long winter, huddled around fires of yak dung. Here are a few Buddhist temples. Trails cross this massive range at the lower passes; and in the summer months great pack trains move south to north, and back again—pack trains of mules and yaks—and of sheep too.

There are very few schools in these mountain valleys and no hospitals. There are no doctors, no movies, no modern conveniences. The people find their entertainment in dancing and singing. Their barren villages look desolate to the eye. But here are tears and laughter, joy and sorrow, hate and love.

My story deals with these peoples, whom I met on my trips to the Himalaya in 1950, 1951 and 1955, as well as with the alpinists who come from the West to climb the peaks.

William O. Douglas

I

THE SNOWS

Himalaya is a Sanskrit word. *Hima* means snow and *alaya,* home. Himalaya is therefore the Home of the Snow.

The Himalaya is a mountain range that runs east and west nearly 2,000 miles. It is the northern border of India and West Pakistan, and its western end cuts through Afghanistan. It has different names in the three countries. In India the range is often referred

3

to as The Snows. It is the highest mountain range in the world. It began to rise nearly fifty million years ago, but the greatest upheaval started fifteen million years ago. Geologists believe it is still rising.

I first saw The Snows from Ranikhet and Almora, hill villages of north central India about 7,000 feet in altitude. The Snows are sixty to eighty miles north of these villages as a crow flies. From Ranikhet and Almora a series of peaks over a hundred miles long can be seen. There are five major ones, of which Nanda Devi (25,643 ft.) is the highest. I have seen these great peaks in the moonlight when their ice fields had a golden glow. At dawn, when the sun first tops the horizon, I have seen a finger of light race across them almost faster than the eye can move. At sunset I have seen the sky behind them turn to gold, to red, to purple. When the sun sets, the colors do not slowly fade. Rather, they seem suddenly to jump into space and disappear. At times the wind blows powder snow from the peak of Nanda Devi, creating the impression that the mountain is smoking. Then the hill people say, "The Goddess Nanda is lighting her kitchen fire."

The eastern flank of The Snows, overlooking Gangtok, capital of the principality of Sikkim, has a different beauty. At this point the high peaks are dominated

4

by Kangchenjunga (28,166 ft.) with Everest (29,028 ft.) in the background. They show to best advantage from Tiger Hill near Darjeeling, the town that is famous for the tea that grows on its steep slopes. At dawn on Tiger Hill one sees the great massif, white with snow and ice, towering high in the sky where one expects to see only clouds. These great peaks loom so high they seem to belong to another world. Some of their glaciers are more than thirty-five miles long.

It was at Darjeeling in northeast India that I first met the Sherpas.

2

THE SHERPAS

The word Sherpas means "Men of the East." They are people of Tibetan stock who live in northeast Nepal, a principality in north India bordering Tibet. They are hill folk who tend yaks, sheep, and goats. Of these the yak is the most important, for it supplies them with wool for clothing, leather for shoes, dung for fuel, and milk, butter, cheese, and meat for food. The tails of the yaks are cut off and sold. They are

9

used for fans in the East and for Santa Claus beards in the West. The Sherpas pasture their yaks at altitudes up to 18,000 feet in the summer. They grow barley and potatoes at altitudes of 14,000 feet and wheat at 10,000 feet.

The Sherpa language is close to Tibetan. So are the clothing, the diet, and the customs of the Sherpas. The Sherpas in Darjeeling cut their hair. But usually Sherpa men follow the Tibetan habit of wearing long, braided hair. Like others of Mongolian stock they have thin beards. Like Tibetans the Sherpas are Buddhists.

Today there is a rather large community of Sherpas living in Darjeeling. The town rests on a high shoulder of the hills, and one slope has been completely taken over by the Sherpas. Their community is a collection of neat wooden houses with tin roofs and tidy garden plots. There is a small Buddhist temple where they worship. It has one small room perhaps fifteen feet square, and most of the space is taken up by a huge drum that revolves on an axis the height of the room. This is a prayer wheel full of prayers written on bits of paper. As it turns, all the prayers are supposed to be said for the worshipers. When the wheel turns a complete round, a gong sounds. There is very little else in the temple except bowls of water on the low mantel that runs around the room. The water is for the spirits who are thought to visit shrines.

Around the corner lives Tenzing Norgay—the most famous of all the Sherpas. He is the one who in 1953 reached the top of Mount Everest with Edmund Hillary of New Zealand.

The Sherpas are sturdy, sure-footed, and well adapted to high altitudes. They always had a native talent for climbing but no special training or experience in scaling the high peaks until 1921, when the British began to train them in alpine climbing.

The British taught the Sherpas how to use crampons—spikes fastened onto shoes for walking on ice and hard snow. They taught them the use of pitons— spikes driven into cliffs for scaling rocks. They showed them how to climb in teams, tied together by ropes so that if one falls the others can hold him or pull him out of a crevasse. The British also explained the art of belaying—how one man climbs to a point, makes an anchor out of himself, and lowers a rope so that others may climb in safety. In the reverse of this method one man, tied to a rope, anchors himself on a slope and braces himself against the fall of those descending a treacherous glacier or snow field.

The British taught the Sherpas how to "read" snow and ice—how to detect soft snow that may conceal a crevasse, how to spot slopes that are dangerous for avalanches, how to walk a cornice of snow along a high ridge. They taught the Sherpas the art of climbing—the way to traverse a slope, the slow rhythmic step as contrasted to the hurried climb. They pointed out the danger of rolling rock, the way to cut steps in ice with an ax, the use of the alpenstock, or staff, as an aid in climbing. The Sherpas also were taught to take care of the sick and injured. And, as important as anything else, they were instructed in all aspects of camp life—cleanliness, cooking, and making camp in high, cold winds.

Other hillmen of the Himalaya are as sturdy and as stalwart as the Sherpas. But none are so well trained. As a result of the British influence, the Sherpas have made a profession of being porters, guides, and climbers. Many have lost their lives in Himalayan expeditions. They are today formed into an association with headquarters at Darjeeling. They have standard rates of pay and a roster of qualified guides. Their association takes care of sick Sherpas, acts as an employment agency, and seeks financial help for Sherpas injured on expeditions and for the families of those who are killed.

Every Himalayan expedition prefers having the Sherpas along. The most successful usually have had them in the party. The Sherpas are extraordinary mountain men. They carry between sixty and ninety pounds at the lower levels and fifty-five pounds when climbing between the higher camps.

The Sherpas have a fine *esprit de corps*. They are proud of their profession and like to be called "Tiger," the name bestowed on them by the British in 1938. More than anything else they prefer being called "Tigers of the Snow."

3

EVEREST AND
ANNAPURNA

The British rule in India ended in 1947. But while they governed there, they did much exploratory work in the Himalaya. Starting in 1830, they made a detailed survey of the peaks. The name of the first Surveyor General was Sir George Everest. The height of Mount Everest was not computed until 1852, when Sir George was no longer in office. But the highest peak was named for him in view of his distinguished record.

To the natives, Everest is Chomolungma, which in Tibetan means "Goddess Mother of the World." The hill people of India would never have dreamed of climbing Everest on their own. For they were raised to believe that it is the home of spirits who would be angry if anyone set foot on its top.

We have long known that Everest and the other Himalayan peaks are dangerous mountains. But we knew that the danger of climbing came not from spirits but from the shortage of oxygen at that high altitude, from the bitter cold, from avalanches of snow, from blizzards, and from treacherous ice falls and crevasses. We also knew that outsiders could not manage an expedition alone; they needed many porters to help them up the mountain. There are no roads through the Himalaya, only trails. All supplies have to be put on the backs of men or animals. Animals are all right for travel in the valleys and along the lower ridges. Only man, however, can scale the icy heights.

Camps must be established at various levels up the mountain. Sleeping bags, gasoline stoves, tents, food and all the miscellaneous equipment that climbers need must be brought to these camps. The lowest camp will be a large one, where everyone's needs can be taken care of. The highest and last camp must be about 28,000 feet, and for two or three men only. The establishment of these camps takes many days of hard climbing.

The British sent their first expedition to Mount Everest in 1921. This expedition was sent only to explore the mountain and find a way up. They did not approach it through Nepal because the government of Nepal would not give them permission to do so. In that year and in subsequent years down to 1950, all attempts to climb Everest were made from the north by way of Tibet, which was reached through Darjeeling. Today Tibet is controlled by Red China, unfriendly to the West. But in the early years, Tibet was a friendly country.

In 1922 the British made their first actual climbing assault on Mount Everest. During that expedition seven Sherpas, roped together, were killed when a great ocean of snow came hurtling off a steep slope.

Many men, both Indian and British, were to lose their lives before Everest was conquered. George Mallory and Andrew Irvine of the 1924 British expedition perished there. They climbed without oxygen, and were last seen less than 1,000 feet from the top of Everest on the northeast ridge. They never returned; and when Hillary and Tenzing reached the top in 1953 there was no trace of Mallory and Irvine except an ice axe. They doubtless slipped and fell on the treacherous ice, catapulting into one of the canyons thousands of feet deep.

The dangers are not merely from slipping and falling. At these high altitudes one's mouth and lungs are so parched they soon become raw and often infected. This happens because the climber inhales cold, dry air and exhales it warm and moist, losing much water in the process. Moreover, the cold is so deep and penetrating that there is always the risk of frostbite, which may mean the loss of toes and fingers. And if one is careless and forgets to use snow glasses, he may become blind for a day or two.

Everest has long been considered a British mountain because the British pioneered in the effort to climb it. Between 1921 and 1953, when Everest was at last climbed by Hillary and Tenzing, eight major expeditions headed toward its top. Most of these were British. Two, however, were Swiss; and the French were planning an assault for 1954 in case the British attempt in 1953 failed.

By 1953 oxygen equipment had been perfected so that it was practical for use in the intense cold one

finds at high altitudes. The British used it not only
for climbing but also for resting and sleeping. Without oxygen one can hardly catch his breath above
26,000 feet. At that level the air contains only about
one-third of the oxygen found at sea level. A tired
man never does get rested. He moves as if he were
drugged. His feet are heavy; his judgment is not good;
he is clumsy and apt to make mistakes. Errors are
apt to be fatal.

George Mallory, who perished on Everest, once said,
"It's an infernal mountain, cold and treacherous."
Eric Shipton, who was one of the few to get within a
thousand feet of the summit, said, "A climber on the
upper part of Everest is like a sick man climbing in a
dream." Frank Smythe, another Britisher who got
close to the top, said that the last thousand feet were
not "for mere flesh and blood."

The 1953 British expedition to Everest under Sir
John Hunt established nine camps on the mountain.
The lowest or base camp was set up at 17,900 feet, the
highest at 27,900 feet. Five men carried the equipment to Camp IX. Hillary and Tenzing remained
there. From that camp they started climbing with
oxygen masks at 6:30 A.M. on May 29, 1953. For most
of their way they had to cut steps in the ice and snow.

Hillary would cut forty steps while Tenzing anchored himself with the rope that was tied to Hillary. Then Hillary would anchor himself and hold the rope while Tenzing climbed the forty steps. Over and over again this procedure was followed. There was a forty-foot rock cliff to scale and no hand holds on it. But on one side they found a narrow crack. Hillary, with his back to the rock and the snow, inched his way up with his crampons and then held the rope taut as Tenzing followed.

From there on, more steps had to be cut to the top. Hillary kept on cutting until he suddenly realized that the ground no longer sloped up. They were at the top of Everest and it was 11:30 A.M.

Tenzing has said that as he stood on top of Everest the mountain resembled a mother hen with all the lesser peaks like chickens under her wing.

Hillary and Tenzing carried the flags of Great Britain, Nepal, India, and the United Nations to the top and left them there. Tenzing also left an offering to the gods—some candy, a red-and-blue pencil his daughter Nima had given him, and a small cloth cat that they had as a mascot. Hillary placed a small crucifix there.

Perfect weather aided the British. But skill, endurance, and careful planning played the greater part. Even so, Hillary and Tenzing barely got off the upper slopes before their oxygen tanks gave out. And for the first thousand feet of the descent they had to cut new steps in the ice and snow, for a fierce wind had already obliterated the ones cut during their ascent.

In 1956 a Swiss expedition climbed Mount Everest twice. Ernst Schmeid and Jurg Marmet reached the top on May 23rd, and Adolph Reist and Hans Von Gunten got there on May 24th.

In 1952 the British had trained for Everest by climbing high on Cho Oyu (26,867 ft.), which is in Nepal, and the sixth highest peak of the Himalaya. There they learned the need for light durable boots for use above 20,000 feet, the best kind of food for high altitude climbing, and the amount of daily fluid intake that is required. They also learned on Cho Oyu how to use oxygen equipment and how to train the climbers for high altitudes. They learned to keep the men at 20,000 feet for only a few days. Then they came down below 13,000 feet for three days; then up again for five days. After three weeks of this training they had good tolerance of high altitudes.

Most Himalayan expeditions have preferred the late Spring for their climbs. But on October 19, 1954, an

Austrian named Herbert Tichy, with Sepp Joehler, a Tyrolese, and a Sherpa, Pasang Dawa Lama, climbed Cho Oyu. That high peak was also climbed by an Indian expedition on May 15, 1958. This was the first Indian success on a major Himalayan peak. The Sherpa, Pasang, was one of the climbers, the other being Sonam Gyaltzen.

One of the greatest human feats ever performed in the Himalaya took place in 1950. On June 3rd of that year a French expedition conquered Annapurna (26,-503 ft.) in Nepal. (Annapurna is a Sanskrit word. *Anna* means corn and *purna* means filled. Annapurna, therefore, means The Bestower of Food.)

Maurice Herzog and Louis Lachenal, who climbed Annapurna without oxygen, were the victorious team. Each suffered from frozen hands and feet. When Herzog took off his mittens at the top, the wind was so strong it blew them away, and he had no pair in reserve. Herzog and Lachenal got back to the highest camp almost frozen. The next day they and the two men waiting for them lost their way and were overtaken by darkness before reaching the lower camp. They spent the second night in an ice cave. The third day they barely reached the second camp before collapsing. Their feet were so badly frozen they could not walk. Sherpas carried them piggyback down the mountain.

During the early stages each crippled climber sat in a basket or sling on a Sherpa's back. Later, the Sherpas made a chair with a long leg rest that could be strapped on a man's back. Still later, stretchers were used. The crippled Frenchmen were carried by Sherpas down treacherous ice and snow fields, over improvised bridges made of tree trunks, up mountains and down again to valleys, through forests, along deep gorges, down slippery grass slopes, and from village to village in the lowlands of Nepal. Herzog and Lachenal owe their lives to the Sherpas. They were carried on the backs of these men for nearly a month.

Herzog and Lachenal suffered greatly during the ordeal. Herzog lost all his toes and every finger but one. Yet he loves the high peaks so much that he still climbs in the Alps.

There are uncounted dozens of Himalayan peaks as high as Alaska's Mount McKinley (20,300 ft.), the highest mountain in America. At least ninety-three Himalayan peaks are over 24,000 feet high, and most of them have yet to be climbed. But of the ten highest Himalayan peaks, all except Dhaulagiri (26,-811 ft.) have now been conquered.

4

KARAKORAM

Karakoram, the name for part of the western flank of the Himalaya, is a Turki word. *Kara* means black and *Koram* means ground covered by large blocks of stone fallen from mountains. Karakoram therefore means Black Rocky Earth. *Kara,* the word for black, describes not color alone but also a mood. It means angry, dangerous, stormy. The Karakoram is indeed dangerous terrain. Its peaks are high; its mountainsides treacherous; its canyons narrow and winding. Many minerals are in the Karakoram, including copper, gold, and marble. Red garnets are also plentiful. Sometimes whole hillsides are so thickly strewn with them that it would be easy to fill a gunny sack.

Six ancient nations or principalities in the Karakoram are now part of West Pakistan. Three of them are in broad valleys approaching the Karakoram— Swat, with 500,000 people, Dir, with 150,000, and Chitral with 100,000. Three others are deeper in the mountains—Gilgit, with 25,000 people, Nagir, with 18,-000, and Hunza with 16,000. Practically all of the people in the Karakoram are Moslems.

At one time this region was largely Buddhist. Buddha lived from about 560 B.C. to 480 B.C. His home was Nepal, and Buddhism became India's religion after his death. Buddhism also spread to Tibet on the north and through the Karakoram into Afghanistan on the west. By the seventh century A.D. Buddhism was strongly entrenched in Afghanistan, as well as in Swat and the other Karakoram principalities. There were many Buddhist temples and some large Buddhist monasteries scattered throughout the region.

The Moslems entered Afghanistan from the west

in the middle of the seventh century A.D. They slew the Buddhist priests and destroyed the temples and monasteries. These Moslem armies were on a religious crusade, converting the people to Islam at the point of the sword and building mosques (churches) where the faithful might worship. By the ninth century A.D. there was not a Buddhist left in Afghanistan.

The Moslem invaders of Afghanistan did not reach the six principalities of the Karakoram. The reason for this is that the Buddhist temples in the Karakoram region were protected by the high mountains. As a result, Buddhism continued to flourish there until the Moslems invaded that mountain fastness in the fifteenth century and razed the temples to the ground.

On my journeys I found relics of the ancient Buddhist shrines in Swat and in the other principalities of the Karakoram. But there are no Buddhists left. Practically all of the people in this region today are Moslems. There are no lamas, no prayer wheels, no pagoda-like temples. In the villages one finds a simple mosque. And everywhere one travels one sees men on their knees, facing east to Mecca and bowing until their foreheads touch the ground. This is the ritual of prayer that a devout Moslem is supposed to perform five times each day. It is practiced both in the farming areas where crops are tilled and on the high crags where flocks of sheep and goats graze.

The valleys of these Karakoram principalities are fairly low in elevation—the Swat Valley being about 2,000 feet high, those of Gilgit and Hunza being about 5,000 feet. But the mountains rise three to four miles from these valleys. It is common to find ridges over 20,000 feet. K2, the highest peak, rises 28,250 feet.

The Swat Valley, which reminded me of our Connecticut valley, grows rice, wheat, barley, and corn; and on its low hills grow many kinds of fruit, from apricots to apples. The higher valleys of Gilgit and Hunza grow many cereals (but no rice), barley being the most common crop. They also grow peas, beans, grapes, and mulberries. The staple fruit is apricots that are dried in the sun and eaten the year around, including the seeds.

Barley and apricots make up the main diet of the people of Gilgit, Nagir, and Hunza. In the summer there are fresh vegetables and, the year around, milk, cheese, and butter from sheep and goats.

Swat has a food surplus. But the other principalities of the Karakoram live on short rations. It is indeed difficult for them to get through a winter without running short of food. The average family has one sheep a year to eat; and they eat it up, including the marrow in the bones, in a week. For the rest of the year they eat only vegetables.

When summer comes and the first crop (which is barley) matures, there is always a festival. There are prayers and music and a service that reminds one of our own Thanksgiving.

Farming in Gilgit, Nagir, and Hunza is done under adverse circumstances. There are few broad fields. Even some of the valleys are practically deserts. The soil is mostly pulverized rock, very porous and with little humus. Some canyons have little water. Most of the farms are on steep mountain slopes where retaining walls have been built to hold terraces a few feet wide. The terraces are a series of steep steps which rise a mile or more above the valley.

When men and women go to the fields to work, they must climb these heights. They carry sheep manure in sacks up the terraces for fertilizers; they carry crops down in baskets. They water the terraces through canals that have been built for miles along these mountainsides. Every available niche of land along the slopes is cultivated up to an elevation of about 10,000 feet.

U.S.S.R.

CHI

HINDU KUSH

AFGHANISTAN

KHYBER
PASS

KARAKORUM

K2

Gilgit

NANGA
PARBAT

KASHMIR

Rudok

BARALACHA
PASS

Patseo

ROTHANG
PASS

Kulu

Simla

NANDA
DEVI

INDUS RIVER

W.

PAKISTAN

Ranikhet

Almora

Delhi

IN

CHINA

TIBET

Lhasa

AREA SHOWN
ON LARGE MAP

Delhi

Calcutta

INDIA

INDIAN
OCEAN

INDIAN
OCEAN

500 MILES

N A

KUNLUN M O U N T A I N S

The Himalaya Mountains run east and west
nearly 2,000 miles. On this map will be found
many of the places mentioned in this book.

T I B E T

◎ Lhasa

HIMALAYA
MOUNTAINS

YAMDROK
TSO

◎ Gyangtse

KANGCHENJUNGA   SIKKIM

HAULAGIRI   BHUTAN

▲ MT.   ◎ Gangtok
ANNAPURNA ▲ ▲ EVEREST

N E P A L   Darjeeling

GANGES RIVER   E.   PAK.

D I A

Calcutta ◎

0   100   200   300

SCALE OF MILES

INDIAN
OCEAN

The hand tool most commonly used is a pick made out of the horn of an ibex. There are many ibex in the Karakoram. The big-horned sheep, called *ovis poli* after Marco Polo, are also found there.

Polo is the sport of these people, particularly in Gilgit, Hunza, and Nagir. Every small village has a polo field. The game is played in a rough manner, the mallet being used to hit one's opponent as well as the ball. The Moslems brought the game to Gilgit, and it was from there that the British exported the game to England.

In the lower reaches of the Karakoram the mountains are mostly barren of trees. At 7,000 feet one finds juniper trees, at 9,000 feet pine and spruce, and birch and aspen up to 10,000 feet. The natives climb high to get juniper for burning. They consider the wood sacred. Its smoke is used to purify a house preceding a wedding, and it is also inhaled for sickness. The bark of the birch and aspen is used to make baskets as well as wrappers for butter and cheese.

There are many earthquakes in the Karakoram. When they come, the ground trembles, houses shake, and there is a great roar of rocks racing down the mountainsides. Then people sit huddled together, hoping and praying the rocks do not come their way.

These avalanches wipe out houses, dam up rivers, and obliterate the terraces where the people farm. The avalanches are caused either by earthquakes or by a chemical change in the mountainsides. The mineral pyrite is common here. Pyrite, wet from rains, forms sulfuric acid; and sulfuric acid dissolves rocks, making them very crumbly. The vibrations of an earthquake or even the hoof of a goat will send tons of earth and rock into a canyon.

The people of the Karakoram are very poor. In Gilgit, Hunza, and Nagir the average person does not have a cash income of more than five dollars a year. They are so poor they seldom can afford tea. Nor can they afford to buy salt. They often get their salt by washing it out of the ground.

Their houses are made of mud and rocks with no chimneys or windows. There is only a hole in the roof over a small fireplace where cooking is done. Here they sit huddled over small fires the long winter through.

There are not many schools in the Karakoram, except for Swat. And most of the schools are for boys only. Apart from Swat, there are few first-aid stations and practically no hospitals worthy of the name. Only trails lead into most of these countries. A jeep road has been built into Gilgit. But the snow closes it for most of the year.

The trails of the Karakoram are treacherous. They are often no more than a narrow ledge along a cliff. Where the ledge ends, the hillmen build a trail out over space. They wedge flat rocks and sticks into cracks along the cliff, forming a narrow platform or gallery. A traveler who crosses these platforms sees daylight between the cracks at his feet and looks down hundreds of feet into an abyss.

There are many rivers to cross in the Karakoram— dark, ugly rivers carrying tons of clay and sand. Sometimes the natives use rafts made of two dozen or more goatskins, which are inflated and tied together in a wooden frame. More often, they cross these rivers of the Karakoram on a rope bridge. Ropes are made by twisting vines and twigs together, and the ends are anchored on a high bank or cliff. Other ropes are stretched across the river waist-high, so that one can hold onto them with his hands while he walks on the footrope. The handrails are tied to the footrope with many smaller ropes.

These rope bridges are usually not in good repair. And when one crosses them in a high wind, they sway in a terrifying way. The natives use them constantly.

But occasionally a rope bridge turns upside down, pitching the passenger into the raging stream below. These rivers are swift—the most treacherous in the world. They can sweep away men and horses alike. When they run full in springtime, they have the roar of grinding rocks in them. The rivers are so powerful one can sometimes see the rocks leaping like fish as they are pushed down steep canyons in great torrents of water.

During the early expeditions into the Karakoram, Sherpas were brought all the way from Nepal to assist the climbers. But Nepal is in India, and in recent years India and Pakistan have not been on friendly terms. So the Sherpas have had difficulty getting into Pakistan. The latest expeditions have therefore used men of Hunza as porters. These men have not had the training of the Sherpas. But they are sturdy mountain men and are beginning to write glorious records in the Karakoram. Hunza porters have already carried crippled climbers out of the rough mountains on their backs and in stretchers.

I flew into Gilgit. The air route goes up the Indus River, which at this point has turned south and cut a deep gorge in the Himalaya. The river runs at the very base of Nanga Parbat which, on the south side, is almost a sheer cliff. The cliff rises nearly four miles above the river. My plane alongside that cliff seemed no bigger than a moth against the tallest New York City skyscraper. Nanga Parbat from the south is terrifying. One who sees it from that side will think it never can be climbed.

Nanga Parbat—which in native tongue means Naked Mountain—is 26,660 feet high. It was finally climbed by a German expedition in 1953, a little more than a month after Everest was climbed. The successful climber was an Austrian, Hermann Buhl, who reached it alone at 7:00 P.M. on July 3, 1953. Darkness soon fell and he had to spend the night high on the mountain. But there was good weather. No howling storms, no avalanches of snow broke loose. And the night was warm so that Buhl suffered no frostbite. He had climbed without oxygen. Breathing at 26,660 feet is almost impossible, and the lack of oxygen depletes the body. One can walk or think only with the greatest difficulty. The lack of oxygen so afflicted Buhl that on the descent he kept seeing people and hearing voices, though no one was present. It was a miracle he got off the mountain alone and unassisted.

Up to 1953 Nanga Parbat claimed the lives of thirty-one climbers—fourteen Europeans and seventeen Indians. The first expedition was sent by the British in 1895, headed by a famous climber, A. F. Mummery. He and two Gurkhas were swept away by an avalanche and never seen again. There was one other British expedition to Nanga Parbat. But the British then concentrated on Everest. Beginning in 1932, the Germans sent a series of expeditions to Nanga Parbat. These suffered a series of defeats and lost a number of climbers. In the 1934 German expedition a Sherpa, Gyali, lost his life in a heroic effort. He could have got down safely. But he stayed behind to take care of Willy Merkl, one of the leaders, and he died with Merkl on the heights. Eight others perished on this disastrous expedition. In 1937, sixteen men were killed in an avalanche on Nanga Parbat.

Hermann Buhl, the man who conquered Nanga Parbat, was probably no better a climber than Willy Merkl, who died there in 1934. Buhl, however, had the fortune of good weather—a calm, clear period for the final assault and the absence of snow conditions that produce avalanches. (The good fortune that followed Buhl in 1953 forsook him later. While climbing the Karakoram in 1957 he fell off a 1,000-foot cliff and his body was never found.)

It was the chance of weather and snow conditions that also spelled the difference between success and defeat in conquering K2 (28,250 feet). The name K2 comes from the location of this mountain on the map. One of its local names is Lamba Pahar, meaning Long Mountain. Its official name is Godwin-Austen, after a Britisher who did much of the survey work in the Karakoram beginning in 1856.

The first expedition to attempt K2 was an Anglo-Swiss-Austrian party in 1902. An Italian expedition explored it in 1909. In 1938 an American expedition led by Dr. Charles S. Houston of Aspen, Colorado, got to 26,000 feet and discovered a feasible way to climb the mountain. The next year another American party, this one headed by Fritz Wiessner, reached a height of at least 27,000 feet on K2. Tragedy followed their footsteps. Dudley Wolfe, an American, became ill on the mountain and he and three Sherpas were lost. The third American expedition, this also under the leadership of Dr. Houston, went to K2 in 1953. It was an excellent team, well conditioned to high altitudes. Dr. Houston—an eminent medical expert—was confident K2 could be climbed without oxygen.

K2 is different from many Himalayan mountains in that it is mostly sheer cliffs with few camp sites that will hold more than two or three small tents. The 1953 expedition made eight camps on tiny shelves up the mountainside. When Camp VIII was established at 25,500 feet, it seemed that victory was within reach. But the morning after the first night at Camp VIII, a storm broke with great fury. It continued for ten days. The wind blew so hard that it blew out the small gasoline stoves *inside the tents*. With no fire, there was no way to melt snow to get drinking water. One tent was ripped open by the wind. There was so much snow in the air that visibility was cut down to fifty or one hundred feet.

Though the men were getting weaker and weaker, they still did not give up hope. Then stark tragedy struck. Art Gilkey, an excellent climber, became seriously ill with a blood clot in his leg. The only alternative was to get him off the mountain. A kind of sled or cradle was made out of a smashed tent and he was wrapped warmly and laced in tightly. At a lull in the storm the party started down.

They were all tied together with nylon ropes. Pete Schoening, who proved to be a great hero, was anchor man. Someone slipped and five experienced climbers fell and went streaking down the mountain, headed for a deep abyss. Schoening braced himself. The nylon rope stretched like a rubber band but did not break. All the men, including Gilkey, were saved. But they were badly bruised and shaken up.

Schoening anchored Gilkey by fastening him to two ice axes that he had driven into the glacier. Then he went to help the injured. It took about forty-five minutes to bind up the wounds and get the injured men back into condition to continue the descent. When they were ready, they went across the slope to get Gilkey. But Gilkey was gone. A great avalanche of fresh snow had swept him off the mountain into a great canyon.

In 1954 an Italian team under the direction of Ardito Desio conquered K2. At the beginning of the climb vicious weather closed in on them. The storm lasted forty days. But the expedition dug in and, when the storms abated, established nine camps up the mountain. The last was at a height of 26,600 feet.

Two members of the team, Lino Lacedelli and Achille Compagnoni, spent a night at Camp IX and on the morning of July 31, 1954, started the final ascent. They used oxygen, and for the final assault each man carried three oxygen cylinders on his back. The weather was good and climbing conditions were favorable. It seemed that they would easily reach the top. But at a point 800 feet below the summit a frightening thing happened. They ran out of oxygen. They gasped for air; they got sleepy; they could hardly move. But they kept on, each taking a few slow steps and then resting. They reached the top only half conscious. After a thirty-minute rest they managed to take some pictures and to plant the flags of Italy and Pakistan on the top.

It was now dark and the awful descent was ahead of them. For four and a half hours they groped their way in the dark on treacherous ice and rock. Compagnoni fell over a fifty-foot cliff but was only bruised. Shortly after, Lacedelli, who was above Compagnoni, also lost his footing and fell over the same cliff. They reached Camp VIII almost crazed from lack of oxygen, and walking like drunken men.

The next morning another terrible storm broke, making it imperative to get off the mountain. Compagnoni and Lacedelli were barely able to walk. But down they went. One of them slipped and was carried 650 feet to the very edge of an 8,000-foot cliff. It was not until August 2nd that both climbers reached safety.

This heroic Italian team, unlike the great American team, was favored by good weather at precisely the right time.

On June 8, 1955, an American team composed of Joseph E. Murphy, Jr., Thomas A. Mutch of Princeton and Major Ken Bankwala of Pakistan conquered Istor-o-Nal (24,242 ft.) in the Karakoram. Murphy and Mutch climbed without oxygen and found, as many alpinists before them had done, that they were seeing exasperating illusions in the form of false summits. Murphy's feet were frostbitten; and after they reached base camp he was carried on a stretcher by porters down the mountain so as to prevent gangrene from infecting his legs.

In 1957 tragedy struck a team of five from the Oxford Mountaineering Club who attempted a climb of Haramosh (24,270 ft.). Two were killed; two suffered severe frostbite. Only Scott D. Hamilton, Jr. of Little Rock, Arkansas, returned alive and well. They made the assault in late August and early September.

After many days of reconnoitering they discovered that Haramosh could not be climbed from the west, the north, or the east. Fresh snow, waist deep, fell while they were about 21,000 feet high on the mountain. At their highest point a snow avalanche swept away two members of the team. By some miracle they survived. But they were now 1,000 feet below two others of the team. The two went down to rescue them. The rescuers got the two out and then themselves became marooned. They spent three days on the glacier. One, Rae Culbert of New Zealand, died of exhaustion. One of the two men they had rescued, Bernard Jillott, of England, fell over a cliff on his return to camp. The two others who survived had severe frostbite, one losing all his toes and fingers.

In one way the Karakoram offers more favorable climbing conditions than the central or the eastern flanks of the Himalaya. There is less rainfall here than in the other sectors. While the eastern Himalaya have 200 or more inches of rain a year, the Karakoram averages around fifteen inches. The Karakoram is drier, with less likelihood of severe storms than the mountains to the east. But the American and Italian experiences on K2 show that the storms that do come are as deadly as those on Mount Everest.

5

THE BLOOD OF THE

KHYBER PASS

Hindu refers to a native of India. Kush means Killer. Hindu Kush means Hindu Killer. The Hindu Kush is a range of mountains to the west of the Karakoram. It is geologically a part of the Himalaya, a western spur that runs into Afghanistan. It got its name in a cruel way.

The Himalaya, running east and west, have served as a great dike protecting India against the north. The north has been filled with conquerors who have had designs on the south and its riches. The conquerors did not, however, bring their armies over the main Himalaya because the passes are too high and are open only a few months each year. They traveled west until they came to the Hindu Kush with its lower passes. Then they turned south.

The Hindu Kush has some high peaks—several over 20,000 feet and Tirich Mir, rising 25,263 feet. The northeastern part of the Hindu Kush is heavily wooded. But the middle section has bare, wind-blown ridges sparsely covered with grass. There are more than a dozen well-traveled passes. Darkot, the highest, is 15,400 feet; Shibar, the lowest, is 9,800 feet. The middle section of the Hindu Kush has the lowest passes, and it was through them that the hordes came down from the north.

Alexander the Great came over the Hindu Kush in 327 B.C. Genghis Khan sent his armies that way in A.D. 1220. Timur followed in 1398.

Babur Khan came down from the north in 1504 and conquered India in 1526. He established the Mogul dynasty that ruled India until the British secured their position in 1764.

The conquerors sacked the temples, raided the

fields, seized the gold and silver, and made slaves out of many Hindus. Those who returned north took their Hindu slaves with them.

Conditioned to the warm weather of the Indian plains, the Hindus suffered greatly from these long journeys. They were accustomed to low altitudes, not to the thin air of high mountains. And they were dressed for the lowlands. The result was that thousands of them became sick and died while crossing the Hindu Kush with their captors. So many died that the mountain range became known as the Killer of Hindus.

Efforts have been made in recent years to give the range a friendlier name. In Persian, the chief language of Afghanistan, Kuh means mountain. So the Afghans have suggested that the mountain range be called Hindu Kuh or Hindu Mountain. But old names are hard to change. Everyone in the region, as well as all the maps and books, still refers to this majestic range as the Hindu Kush.

Though the major invaders of India came over the Hindu Kush from the north, others came from the west. Beginning A.D. 1000 Mahmud of Ghazni, an Afghan, sent many armies against India. He was a Moslem, waging a religious war. His aim was to convert the people to the Moslem faith. He did indeed convert to Islam most of northwest India—the part that today is West Pakistan. In 1738 Nadir Shah of Persia came to India on a raiding expedition. His army looted Delhi and carried the famous Peacock Throne back to Iran.

These invading armies, whether coming down from the north or in from the west, usually poured through a famous low pass in a range of hills running north and south. Today this range of hills marks the border between West Pakistan and Afghanistan. The pass is called the Khyber. It's a low notch—only 3,518 feet high—in dry barren hills. The notch is actually a narrow, twisting canyon thirty miles long. The canyon is from forty to a few hundred feet wide. Cliffs rise a thousand feet above the road. There is no water in the Khyber. It's a barren, not a green, defile. It has no trees. Even bushes are few and far between. The canyon is filled with great rocks. It is a furnace in summer.

The Khyber is not only the funnel through which the invaders of India poured. It is also the great caravan route linking both India and West Pakistan to Afghanistan. When I visited the Khyber, I saw caravans made up of hundreds of camels, horses, and burros.

The people who live in the hills surrounding the Khyber are called Pathans. They are ancient tribes— the Afridis, Wazirs, Mahsuds, Shinwaris, Bajawaris, Baluchis, and Mohmands. They raise some grain, but they are mostly herders of sheep and goats. They winter their flocks around the Khyber. In the summer they take them high into the Hindu Kush.

The Pathans are a hardy lot, and they fought every invader who came through the Khyber. They were long a thorn in the side of the British, who first placed a military fort in the pass in 1839. The Pathans raided that fort; their snipers shot down British sentries; they stole British guns and copied them in their secret arsenal in the hills. They also stole British supplies and generally made life uncomfortable for the British. Much British blood was shed in the Khyber. That is where Kipling wrote his famous poem, "Arithmetic on the Frontier." Winston Churchill served there as a young British officer.

The Khyber produced many British heroes. And the Pathans—tall lean men with high cheekbones and prominent noses—produced heroes of their own. The

Pathans are Moslems and made the defense of the Khyber a holy affair. They erected a mosque in the Khyber. Ali, the son-in-law of Mohammed, is said to have ascended from the Khyber to heaven on a great white horse. When I visited the Khyber, Pathans showed me marks on the rocks which are supposed to be the prints made by the hoofs of his horse—half flying, half running, and touching the ground only now and then. Since the Khyber was a holy place to the Pathans, they defended it ferociously.

So it is that the main Himalaya, the Karakoram, and the Hindu Kush have each played an important role in the history of India. They have largely separated the peoples of the north from those of the south. But in one stretch of the great barrier close cultural ties have been established and maintained between the peoples on both sides. I speak of the 800-mile range of the Himalaya in India where Tibet is the northern neighbor. India and Tibet have long been at peace. The cultural ties between them have been strong because of the influence of the Buddhist religion. The Tibetan people have been the most fascinating to those who travel the Himalaya.

6

SHEEP CARRY THE
FREIGHT

I crossed the Himalaya near the end of their western reach in India. I had not been on the trail many days before I saw my first sheep train, loaded with salt, coming down from Tibet.

This was a band of 1,500 sheep led by a billy goat named Tashi. They were under the charge of Thundup and Phuti, father and daughter respectively, who lived in far-off Rudok in western Tibet. Phuti and Tashi led the sheep. Thundup, riding a pony, brought up the rear.

Phuti was a beautiful Mongol girl of fourteen with coal-black hair in a long braid, high cheekbones, deep-set brown eyes, and dark-yellow skin. When I first saw her she was sitting on a huge rock dangling her feet in clear, cold water that came gushing off the mountainside. She wore a sheepskin on her back. It was a cape held by a string around her neck; the wool side of the skin was next to her back. The cape protected her from the wind by day and it was her blanket at night.

In appearance the sheep in her band were much the same as the sheep of America, though they had longer legs and were quite skinny. Each sheep had two small burlap bags of salt fastened like packs on its back and made secure by a flat cloth band running under the belly, just like a cinch on a horse.

The weight an animal can carry in the Himalaya is called a *khal*. A proper *khal* for a sheep does not exceed thirty-two pounds. These sheep did not have more than twenty pounds of salt each. Thundup had loaded them fairly light because of the long journey. The Tibetan salt was to be traded for Indian goods. The bags that held the salt on the way south would hold grain on the return trip.

About noon Tashi, the goats and Phuti had led the band over Baralacha Pass, which is 16,200 feet high. On Baralacha, as on other high Himalayan passes, there are piles of rock into which travelers have stuck flags. These rock piles are called *obos*. The flags, made of cotton cloth, have prayers printed on them. And the belief is that every time the flag flutters the prayer is said. A traveler has the prayer said for him by making an offering such as food or a flower at the site. If he has no gift to deposit, he always adds a rock to the pile as he passes.

This day on Baralacha both Thundup and Phuti added stones to the *obos*. There was fresh grass there. But Phuti did not let the sheep tarry since Thundup got sick at high altitudes. He got sick because of the thinness of the air. But he believed he got sick because the pass was poisonous, because evil spirits lived there who made people sick to keep them away.

The trail off Baralacha leads down a narrow winding canyon that takes two hours to travel. It opens into a wide treeless basin where only a few dandelions grow in summer. At this place Phuti stopped the band

and sat on a rock while the sheep scattered for grazing.

In a few minutes Thundup joined her. Thundup was past fifty and somewhat old for his years. He, too, was barefoot and his toes were like talons. His black trousers were frayed. His brown coat—which served for a shirt as well and reached almost to his ankles—was woven of coarse wool. His hat was made of brown cloth and had no brim. He dismounted from his pony and sat next to Phuti, leaning on one elbow and picking his white teeth.

They decided they had come far enough this day. Though it was only mid-afternoon, they would camp as soon as they reached water. That was only a mile away, where the trail touched the Bhaga River.

7

SALTY TEA AND
UNLEAVENED BREAD

I camped with Thundup and Phuti at a level spot by the Bhaga River. They took the pack bags off the sheep and piled them along three sides of a square, the open side facing the south. The bags made a wall nearly six feet tall, high enough for a good windbreak. There was little danger of rain, for on the north side of the Himalaya precipitation is about eight inches a year. As Thundup piled the salt bags, Phuti gathered fuel. There were no trees; a low dark bush called the *dama* was the only fuel available. But it is excellent for fires since it burns even when green.

The supper of these Himalayan travelers was the same as their breakfast: *gur gur cha, sattu,* and *chapattis.*

Gur gur cha requires a kettle and a wooden churn; *chapattis,* a convex copper plate; and *sattu,* cups. Thundup had a small copper kettle holding two quarts. The churn was a cylinder four inches wide and fifteen inches long, fitted with a plunger. The convex copper plate was about eighteen inches in diameter. The cups were crude metal ones.

Thundup, who started his fire with a piece of flint, put water in the churn, added several pinches of salt, and a piece of yak butter about the size of an egg. Using the plunger, he churned these ingredients vigorously for a few minutes and then dumped the contents of the churn into the kettle of water. When the kettle came to a boil, he added tea. After the tea had settled, he poured a cup for himself and one for Phuti.

Holding his cup in his two hands, Thundup watched Phuti make *chapattis,* an Indian dish not much used in Tibet proper. She took coarse flour made from millet, mixed it with water and kneaded the dough in her hands until it was just the right texture. Then with the quickness that only Tibetan women have, she stretched the dough across the palms of her two outstretched hands and dropped it quickly onto the copper plate. When bubbles appeared on the top side of this thin, unleavened bread, she lifted it carefully by a corner and turned it. When it was done, she laid it by the fire and started another.

Thundup, having sipped his cup of *gur gur cha*, made his *sattu*. Before leaving home, Phuti had roasted several sacks of barley over an open fire and ground the barley with a pestle made of rock. This cooked flour or *sattu* (known in Tibet proper as *tsamba*) was the mainstay of every meal. It needed no additional cooking. Thundup mixed it with his *gur gur cha,* and when a thick paste was formed, he ate it with his fingers.

The *chapattis* made up the last course. This night, because the fire was good, Phuti made a large batch of them. She made enough for tomorrow's breakfast and tomorrow's lunch. Cold *chapattis* would in fact be all there was for lunch the next day.

8

A HIMALAYAN GHOST

The morning star hung low over Baralacha Pass and it was still pitch-dark when Thundup woke Phuti. He had a hot cup of *gur gur cha* ready when she returned from washing in the ice-cold river. Breakfast was soon over and it was decided that Phuti should take the sheep—and the pony, too—to a high basin for grazing. Thundup would wait in camp. The animals

71

needed good grazing for they had lived on small nibbles for some days.

Stuffing some *chapattis* in her pockets, Phuti started Tashi up the ridge to the east of camp. The sheep followed and Phuti brought up the rear on the pony. By daybreak the band was over 500 feet above the valley. Our camp was at an altitude of 13,000 feet. The meadows where Phuti was headed were between 16,000 and 17,000 feet. It had been daylight for more than two hours before the sun shone on the slope that Phuti climbed. The sun had a 25,000-foot barricade of the Himalaya to surmount.

The grass of the high meadow was young and tender. It was dotted with yellow violets, bluish geraniums, dark-hued poppies, and red cinquefoil. Phuti stretched out on a huge rock in a sunny spot. Above her a sheer cliff rose a mile or more. It had three frozen falls hanging like gray gargantuan beards down its side. These icicles, nearly a mile long, hung from glaciers that topped the high ridge. The ice falls dripped at their tips, keeping the meadow moist.

A few marmots frisked about their holes, whistling at Phuti and behaving like mischievous boys. Three ibex crossed a saddle on the ridge above her. Farther down the mountainside a herd of wild asses were making for another saddle. They were as big as good-sized mules with long tails. They had light-tan bodies and dark-brown splotches on their backs and heads.

This is the land of the snow leopard. Phuti kept scanning the heights for one. But she saw none. This is also the place where brown wolves roam, looking for sheep. But Phuti was not afraid since wolves attack only at dusk or in the night. By then she would be back at camp.

On the high cliffs above Phuti, Hilda Richmond, an American, had been killed while climbing. This was years ago. But Phuti had heard the tale and wondered if the white lady had been killed by evil spirits.

The lamas and Thundup had taught Phuti to be superstitious. She was sure there were demons everywhere. The lamas had told her that the good gods, whose pictures hung in the temple at the monastery, were ferocious so as to scare away the evil ones. They told her there were demons that made people faint, others that gave them headaches, some that caused cramps. When a man turned his ankle, it was the devil that had hit him. When a woman had a stomach ache or dysentery, the devil had seized her. Phuti once saw a sick woman lie on her back and put a live coal on

73

her stomach. Then she had a friend blow on the coal until it was red hot in order to get rid of the demon.

Phuti was taught that some spirits live in lakes and have to be appeased by drowning someone every year. Toss a stone into one lake and there will be rain. Disturb the waters of another lake and pestilence will descend on a village. Near Lhasa a witch is buried, and the power of the witch is still so strong that she raises part of her head out of the ground every day.

Then there are the *ro-langs*. A *ro-lang* is a person who has been killed by lightning. The body stands upright and walks with eyes straight ahead. No one can make a *ro-lang* change direction. If anyone touches a *ro-lang,* he becomes sick and dies.

Phuti ate her *chapattis* at noon and took a nap. Then she went about the meadow collecting long-stemmed wild flowers and weaving them into a garland for her hair. When the sun indicated it was about three o'clock, she located Tashi and started him down the mountainside toward camp. Then she herded the sheep and the pony behind Tashi until they were all moving.

Phuti stayed behind, climbing a small pinnacle as she watched the sheep below her. Then the shock came—first fright, then sheer terror that sent her tumbling off the rock and running like a deer.

Phuti had heard a slight noise and turned suddenly to see a strange character standing near the rock. It was over six feet high, very skinny, with long scarecrow legs and dangling arms. It was so brown as to be almost black. The head was thin and oval, the hair dark and stringy. The nose was like a hook. The eyes were deep-set and stared straight ahead. It was naked except for a coarse garment wound around its loins and thrown over its shoulders. Phuti was certain it was a *ro-lang,* and that if it touched her she would die.

She ran so fast she soon passed the band of sheep. As she ran she thought she could feel the breath of the *ro-lang* on her neck. She thought every step would be her last. Suddenly she fell, tripping over a rock and skinning her knee. She looked up and found herself alone. The *ro-lang* had disappeared.

Phuti told the story to Thundup that night at camp. When she had finished, Thundup put his arm on her shoulder and said:

"My child, you should not have been frightened. What you saw was a *Gaddis*—a man from the plains of India who brings goats and sheep to these mountains in the summer. The Gaddis are strange looking, but they are kind people. In the morning we will probably see his flocks high above us."

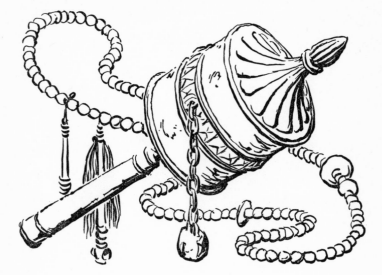

9

A PRAYER WHEEL

During Phuti's absence a number of new people with pack trains of mules had joined our camp. The mules had been carrying bales that now were piled in horseshoe-shaped walls enclosing the new camps. Most of the bales contained wool, much of it goat's wool that comes from one region up north and is finer than any other wool in all the Himalaya. It is used to make the famous Kashmir, or Cashmere, scarves and shawls.

Some of the bales contained tea from China. This tea had been chopped fine, steamed in tubs, partially dried, mixed with enough rice water to make it sticky, and then pressed tightly into hard bricks for mule transport. There were piles of Tibetan blankets, bundles of wild onions that Indian cooks use for seasoning, skins of the marmot and fox, and packages of borax and musk.

At dusk the mules were brought to camp and tied up. The muleteers did not want to climb the peaks in early morning looking for their animals. These mules were hitched in the usual Himalayan way. Two stakes were driven into the ground and a chain was stretched between them along the ground. As many as a dozen mules were tied to one chain. There was much biting and kicking. But soon the animals settled down for the night.

Thundup and Phuti joined the muleteers around a fire. There were about a dozen men, all told, and one other woman, the wife of a muleteer. She and Phuti kept the *gur gur cha* hot and the cups full. One muleteer had a small guitar and he played and sang beautifully. He sang of old Tibetan kings and of the lamas who lived in the big monasteries at Lhasa. The song the crowd liked best was about a man who was accused of being a lama. The accused went to great lengths to prove he was *not* a lama. Everyone always laughed at that song because in the Himalaya the most important person *is* a lama.

One of the muleteers had a flute with which he could produce wonderful effects. He made the sound of water falling off a high Himalayan cliff. It was haunting music.

Another muleteer had a prayer wheel which Phuti admired. It was a silver cylinder about two inches in diameter and four inches long, inscribed with gold. The cylinder was fastened to a twelve-inch handle by a wire axle. A twist of the wrist twirled the cylinder. A silver chain about two inches long with a silver ball at the end was attached to the edge of the cylinder to give it momentum. A prayer wheel is always turned clockwise.

When the muleteer walked the trail, he changed the prayer wheel from one hand to the other, keeping it constantly turning. He stopped only to do his chores and eat his dinner. He had written prayers on paper and stuffed the cylinder with them. His twirling sent thousands of prayers for him and his family wafting their way to heaven.

Phuti liked the feel and the balance of this prayer wheel. Also, it was more beautiful than any she had ever seen. The gold inscription was the sacred Buddhist mantra or chant, *Om Mani Padme Hoom,* meaning "O Jewel of the Lotus." The beautiful lotus flower often grows in filthy places. It adorns the hut of the poorest man as well as the castle of the rich. The legend is that Buddha was born in a lotus. Buddha, like the lotus, showed how goodness can come out of misery and oppression.

Before going to bed Phuti whispered in Thundup's ear, "Daddy, maybe you can buy me a prayer wheel."

Thundup figured that the only way he could afford a fine prayer wheel would be to trade some of his salt for snuff. Snuff-taking is as common in Tibet as smoking is in the West. In Tibet snuff is in great demand and is worth almost its weight in silver.

10

A HIMALAYAN FAIR

We made camp at Patseo before dark the next night. Patseo, which means Stone Bridge, is a bleak and barren flat spot on a bench above the Bhaga River. It is 12,400 feet in elevation, just above the junipers which fill the lower canyon of the Bhaga.

There was shade at Patseo but only in the tents the traders had set up. These were mostly pieces of canvas or cloth stretched above poles to form flat roofs.

85

Under these roofs a great supply of goods was on display. While caravans came down from Tibet, other caravans came up from the valleys of India to meet at Patseo. Patseo is an ancient market place on one of the oldest Himalayan trails—perhaps several thousand years old. Its August fair is famous in Himalayan trade circles.

Thundup and Phuti had hard work cut out for them. They first had to shear by hand the 1,500 sheep in their band and bale the wool for weighing and handling. They then had to weigh the wool and measure the salt and start the long process of bargaining for the supplies they wanted to take back to Tibet. They had also been instructed to sell most of the sheep and return to Tibet with Tashi and not more than 300 ewes.

The sheep were for the most part not owned by Thundup. Only ten ewes were his. The rest, as well as Tashi, belonged to the lamas. They, in fact, owned the five acres of land that Thundup tilled. He was a sharecropper, renting the land from the lamas, growing barley, and raising a few chickens. In addition to the sheep he had a half-dozen goats that he used primarily for cheese. Phuti also got soft wool from the goats. This

Beyond the sloping hills of Darjeeling tower the white peaks of Everest and Kangchenjunga.

From their open-fronted shops the Indian merchants of
Ranikhet look out on the distant Himalayas.

Native porters depart on the 1953 Everest expedition. Each one carries a forty-pound bundle.

"Tiger" Tensing, who scaled the peak of Everest with Sir
Edmund Hillary, is the most famous of all Sherpas.

On their way to the base camp, porters of the 1953 Everest expedition move up the "trough" between large ice pinnacles.

Opposite: Hillary leads a Sherpa climber over the broken ground of an icefall. The knee-deep snow and hidden crevices are extremely dangerous.

Below: In 1954 an Italian mountain-climbing expedition finally conquered the formidable K2, second highest peak in the world.

(United Press)

Above: A caravan plods along a mountain-rimmed plain in Kashmir.

Below: This Tibetan *chhorten* marks the burial place of an important man.

The celebrated Khyber Pass affords the most accessible route through the Hindu Kush mountain range. (Chapter 5)

(United Press)

Above: Two Tibetan lamas—a young Rinpoche and an elderly Lobon—preside over a religious dance. (Chapter 17)

Below: This Tibetan *mani* wall is topped by flat rocks on which religious words have been chiseled. (Chapter 13)

The temple of Kundelin, near Lhasa, is one of the four out-
standing temples in Tibet.

The facial features of this Tibetan family bear a resemblance
to those of the American Indian.

she spun into yarn and from the yarn she wove by hand most of their clothing.

Thundup had never been to school, but he knew simple arithmetic, and he was shrewd and intelligent. The lamas said he was the best bargainer in southwest Tibet.

The lamas owned the salt that was in the pack bags on the sheep. Thundup and Phuti had dug it from the shores of a salt lake in southwest Tibet. It was not pure salt, for it had some dirt in it. But it would bring a high price because of its quality.

The saying at Patseo is that five sheeploads of salt are the equivalent of four sheeploads of barley and corn. The salt would be exchanged in part for corn. The lamas were particularly anxious that each of the 300 ewes making the return trip bring back to Tibet at least 20 pounds of corn. There were 500 lamas to feed in this monastery and 6,000 pounds of corn would help greatly in seeing them through the long Tibetan winter.

The rest of the salt and all of the wool would be traded for goods, not food. And the sheep would be sold for cash. Thundup was authorized to find a young mule and purchase it if the price was right.

The lamas would pay Thundup and Phuti for their three months' work. How much, Thundup did not know. One year he did so well in his bargaining with the Indian traders that the lamas paid him 150 rupees ($30.00) for his three months' trek. That was more money than Thundup had ever before had as his own. It was more cash—three times more—than a Tibetan farmer sees in any one year. Thundup hoped to earn as much this year.

It took Thundup and Phuti most of a week to shear the sheep. There was no great rush, for all the Indian traders had not arrived at Patseo. They came by pack train from the south. It's a five- or six-day trip with mules over Rothang Pass, which is 13,200 feet high. Rothang is one of the most dangerous Himalayan passes. Great storms make up there. The name Rothang means Death.

By the end of the week Patseo was a beehive of activity. Hundreds of bales of wool, thousands of sacks of salt, were piled high. Huge scales for weighing bulky products were built like teeter-totters, the wool or salt being suspended on one end and the weights of measurement on the other. The wool was weighed and classified according to quality. So was the salt. The hides were sorted. The bricks of tea were unpacked for sampling. The other Tibetan products were made ready for display to the Indian merchants.

These Indian traders were a match for the Tibetans. They would refuse an offer one day if there was a chance for a rupee more the next day. Each sat under his canvas with his wares on display.

The Indian traders offered cotton prints of all colors and design, Kashmir woolen scarves, caps, boots, shoes, and slippers. They displayed fountain pens and ink, pocket watches and wrist watches. There were tins of beef and fruit, many sacks of rice, wheat, flour, and chickpeas. Axes, hammers, saws, pocketknives, butcher knives, table forks and spoons, aluminum cups, and kerosene lanterns and cans of kerosene were for sale. Counters were covered with Indian spices. There were hair ornaments, earrings, and bracelets on display. There were also ankle bracelets and rings for the nose and beautiful necklaces of stones that looked like sapphires. What fascinated Phuti the most were cans of talcum powder, jars of perfume, and bottles of hair oil.

Thundup, too, was window-shopping. He saw some Indian slippers he badly wanted. A pocketknife caught his eye. But best of all was the Indian snuff.

II

INDIAN BOY AND
TIBETAN GIRL

At Patseo Phuti met an eighteen-year-old Indian boy named Murli Dhar, who had come to the fair with his father and a caravan of horses over Rothang Pass. Murli Dhar had helped his father set up the tent and unpack the goods. He had risen early the next morning and taken the horses to a high meadow above Patseo where he had left them to graze. On his way down he met Phuti herding her sheep on a lower bench. He shouted to her and went running to meet her. This time Phuti was not scared. In fact, when Murli Dhar smiled and shouted the customary Tibetan words of greeting, *"Ju Le, Ju Le,"* Phuti returned the smile and felt happy inside.

Murli Dhar (which means flute bearer) was tall, sturdy, and well built. He had big strong hands. His head was well formed, though his neck was a bit long and his ears a bit big. But his lips had a constant smile around them, and his brown eyes were always warm. This was the sixth trip he had made to Patseo with his father. They usually stayed a month. His father spoke Tibetan well, and the month spent each summer at Patseo made Murli Dhar fairly fluent in the language.

Murli Dhar saw Phuti every day until Thundup closed all his bargains and started the sheep train back to Tibet. Their hours together were spent in part by Phuti's telling Murli Dhar of her faraway village beyond the Indus River in southwest Tibet. But most of the time was taken by Murli Dhar's stories about the people of India who lived south of Rothang Pass in the Kulu Valley.

He told her of the fish they catch in the Kulu Valley. Phuti knew about trout, for there are trout in a few high Himalayan streams. But she never dreamed of fish like the *mahsir* that look somewhat like our salmon and weigh up to sixty pounds.

Phuti knew about apricots. But the other fruits Murli Dhar mentioned—cherries and peaches—were strange to her.

Murli Dhar described the forests and the wild flowers that grew south of Rothang Pass. Rothang is on the first main ridge of the Himalaya. It is this ridge that catches most of the rain clouds that come with the monsoon in June from the Indian Ocean. These clouds spend themselves on the main ridge, spilling most of their water on the south side. The south side, therefore, is green and lush.

The village where Murli Dhar lived is 6,000 feet in elevation. It is a comfortable place in the summer and never really cold in the winter. Murli Dhar told Phuti of the cornfields and rice paddies in the hill country of northern India. Almost any vegetable would grow there. He pointed to one of his feet to show how big the potatoes were.

Murli Dhar had been to the plains of India with his father many times and had seen how flat and hot they were. They were covered by vast expanses of cotton, hemp, wheat, and millet. Between the plains

95

and the mountains he had seen the jungle where the grass grows twenty feet high. This was where the tigers, elephants, and snakes were. He and his father stopped to trade at many villages between the mountains and the plains. In these villages he picked up stories of man-eating tigers and boa constrictors so big they could strangle a sheep. He liked the jungle even less than the plains. And he was always happy to get back to the hills and out of the humidity and oppressive heat.

There is good hunting in the Indian hills that lie at the foot of the Himalaya. They are filled with bears, leopards, wildcats, hyenas, foxes, porcupines, ibex, and deer. Wealthy Indians—and Europeans, too—often come to the hills to hunt. Once Murli Dhar helped pack some of these hunters into the mountains.

Murli Dhar was a Hindu, and the Hindus have several temples in the Kulu Valley. These temples are pagoda-like structures which usually stand in a forest of deodar trees. Deodar trees, Murli Dhar explained, are holy trees because spirits live in them. Each Hindu temple has at least one spirit. People pray to the god or goddess, and when they finish they pound a nail into a deodar tree. Most Hindu temples have a *chela* or oracle who can tell what the god or goddess wants.

They are supposed to be able to get the spirit to cure a sick child, to send a plague away, or to make it rain. The people honor their gods or goddesses by processions in which a small statue of the spirit is carried on a platform held shoulder-high by four men. Dancers go ahead of the procession; an orchestra of drums and flutes brings up the rear.

Murli Dhar had a small flute and played many songs for Phuti. The songs were mostly about love, but one tune that set her toes wiggling was about war. There was another that she whistled all the way back to Tibet. It was a song about a girl who was in love with a boy, Kunjva. All that Phuti could remember was the last line, "Kunjva, my camp is in the plains of Chamba. Come at night time."

Patseo is located in Lahul, a province of India in the Himalaya. The Lahulis are Tibetan in appearance. They do not, however, give their women as much freedom as Tibetan women enjoy. The women of Lahul always work the fields, while the men sit under the trees supervising them. Phuti asked Murli Dhar about this. He told her that Hindu women have equal rights with men. Thus the Lahuli women always like to leave their own province to marry a Hindu in the Kulu Valley, where they are better treated.

Murli Dhar talked so much about women of the Himalaya leaving the high basins to marry Hindus in the lower hills that Phuti felt at times he was talking directly to her. She was almost certain of it the last night at Patseo, for Murli Dhar gave her as a farewell present gold earrings with thin medallions the size of a dollar hanging down.

12

THE COMMUNISTS
INVADE TIBET

Neither Phuti nor Murli Dhar had ever read Kipling's *Kim*. Phuti couldn't read, for she had never been to school. In Tibet there are no schools for children. There are primary schools in the Kulu Valley, and Murli Dhar had been through four grades. But he had never heard of *Kim*. If Phuti and Murli Dhar had known the book, they would have thought that the

lama who appeared at Patseo had stepped right out of
it.

This lama had traveled some of the same Himalayan
trails as the lama in *Kim*. Like him, he was tall, robed
in heavy red garments, and wore a wooden rosary
around his waist. His face was wrinkled and his voice
was soft. Like the lama in the book, he was on a pilgrimage. The lama in *Kim* was in search of the holy
river where one could bathe and lose all his sins. The
lama at Patseo was on his way to a famous Buddhist
shrine in India, south of the Himalaya. He had come
down from Tibet on a circuitous route, because a bene-
factor and friend had brought him a good part of the
way with a caravan.

The traders at Patseo—Indian and Tibetan alike—
took care of the lama during his sojourn. He was a
holy man to whom everyone on a Himalayan trail
gives food, a place to sleep, and alms.

Everyone in Patseo knew that Red China had its
army stationed in Tibet. But this lama explained that
Tibet was not properly a province of China, that
Tibet's great struggle had been to be free and independent of China. Tibet is China's western neighbor.
It was taken over by China about A.D. 1700. But
whenever China was weak, the Tibetans arose and put

the Chinese out of the country. Whenever China was strong again, she sent her armies to reconquer Tibet. During World War II, while China was busily engaged against the Japanese, Tibet was independent. When China was taken over by the Communists, Tibet was at once endangered. In 1951 the Red Chinese army invaded Tibet, taking over the entire country.

The lama went on to say that the people of Tibet did not welcome the Red Chinese. Neither did the lamas. The Communists do not believe in God. The lamas feel that any group which is antireligious is not to be trusted. This wandering lama reported that the Red Chinese were building roads across Tibet, linking it up with Russia on the west and China on the east. He reported that more and more of Tibet's trade was going to China on the east rather than to India on the south. One of the Indian traders spoke up to say that there were not nearly as many caravans coming down from Tibet now as there had been before Red China invaded Tibet.

In 1954 India and China made a trade treaty which included trading with Tibet. But the Tibetan trade has not greatly increased. The lama said his merchant friends in Lhasa told him that for every three caravans that used to go to India, there was only one now.

The Indian traders agreed that the existing trade was only a third of the old trade.

The lama brought other news. The Red Chinese were building public schools in Tibet. In its long history Tibet had had no public schools. The only schools were for the lamas in the monasteries. Any boy might become a lama and any girl a nun. But no child was educated unless he or she became a member of a religious order. The lama at Patseo thought that every child should be educated. He feared, however, that the new schools in Tibet would educate the children in the communist way of life.

The lama said that India should have a school program for her Himalayan areas. He estimated that in Tibet there were about a million and a quarter people, while in India's Himalayan regions there were between twelve and fourteen million. These people should be educated, the lama said, so that they could better combat the Communists.

At this point an Indian, who from his beard and tightly wound turban was plainly a Sikh, pushed his way to the front of the group. He was the Tehsildar, or civilian officer, in charge of Lahul, representing the Indian government. He told the group that the lama was right, that India's hill people needed education, that schools were necessary to combat communism. He went on to say that, from Lahul in the west to Sikkim on the east, public schools for all Himalayan children were being built. He thought that in ten years every Himalayan child in India would have a school to go to.

13

A LONELY GIRL

It took Thundup and Phuti more than a month to make the return trip to Rudok. All the way home Phuti was lonesome with thoughts of Patseo. Before leaving the fair she had had her ears pierced by an Indian trader and she wore Murli Dhar's earrings. She missed him very much and hoped that the lamas at the monastery would send Thundup to Patseo another year.

It was October and the chill of winter was in the air when Thundup and Phuti arrived home with 300 sheep, the pony, and a new mule. Only when she was within ten miles or so from Rudok was Phuti glad she had come home. Now there were familiar sights that brought back memories of her childhood. As she came around a bend, she saw the town. The houses were in tiers along a steep slope. An old palace of a prince stood at the top of the hill. Near the top was a monastery—the monastery for which Thundup worked. It was painted white with red and black stripes around the top.

Ahead by the side of the trail was a famous *chhorten* thirty feet tall, round at the base, whitewashed, and pointed at the top where a copper moon had been placed. This *chhorten* honored a Tibetan merchant of the last century who was known for his charity. A *chhorten* is a holy place, for in it some part of the deceased is buried—a lock of his hair, his ashes, or one of his bones. A *chhorten* is a place where spirits gather. When people pass a *chhorten*, they always keep it on their right. For there is an ancient Tibetan saying, "Beware of the devils on the left-hand side."

When they reached this *chhorten*, Thundup and

Phuti stood aside to let a funeral procession pass. The body of the deceased was on a stretcher, covered with cloth. Lamas were in front, chanting as they walked; relatives followed the body; an orchestra of drums and flutes brought up the rear. The funeral procession marched once around the *chhorten,* clockwise, and then headed up the mountain to a favorite spot where huge rocks formed a large, flat platform. Here the body would be laid out and the lamas would call the vultures to eat it. When the bones had been picked clean, they would be crushed, mixed with meal, and formed into balls. Then the vultures would be called again.

Cremation of the body is preferred in Tibet. But fuel is scarce. So the vultures are often used instead. It is important, the lamas say, that the body be destroyed at death. For only in that way can the spirit escape. It is important for the spirit to escape the body after death because Buddhists, like Hindus, believe in reincarnation. According to their theory, the spirit of the deceased enters the body of a newborn child and possesses it, thus starting life over again. One never dies; his spirit possesses a new body at the end of each lifetime.

Thundup and Phuti next came to a *mani* wall. They had passed many *mani* walls on their long trek. Most of them were only a few yards long. But some in Tibet are a mile or more long. The one that Thundup and Phuti now approached was almost a half-mile long. It was five feet high, twelve feet wide, and made of rocks. The rocks were loosely piled, not cemented, but they were neatly arranged to make a wall of smooth sides and trim corners.

The top of the wall was covered with flat rocks, and on each one a lama had engraved with a chisel the sacred words, *Om Mani Padme Hoom*. One keeps a *mani* wall on his right as he passes. If he does that, all of the prayers engraved on the rocks are said for him. And one murmurs over and over again as he passes the wall, *Om Mani Padme Hoom*.

Beyond the *mani* wall were *tharchens* or flags nailed high on long poles. There were about two dozen of them. Most of them honored dear ones who had died. Some commemorated historic events, such as the visit to the village of an Incarnate Lama. Phuti's mother, Dolma, had died when Phuti was ten. Phuti saw the red flag Thundup had raised in Dolma's memory. He had had a lama print a Buddhist prayer on the cotton cloth. Then he had fastened the banner to a pole and raised it.

Jigmet, the older brother of Phuti, was waiting for them at their home. He greeted Thundup first. Then he hugged Phuti. Jigmet was obviously excited and delighted at having them back home. He had worried for fear Thundup might have been ill. Most Tibetan men are of medium size, but Jigmet was tall and rangy, topping six feet. He helped unload the sacks of corn from the sheep and the packs from the pony and the mule.

Most Tibetan houses are two-storied, with the animals on the ground floor and the family upstairs. Thundup's home was different. It was a one-story affair made of stone and mud with rafters of poplar wood. The ceiling was six feet high. The flat roof was made of poles covered with rocks and mud. There was, of course, no plumbing. In a merchant's home in Tibet the floors would be of wood, and thick pillows would be used for chairs. The tables would be individual ones —small, lacquered, and standing about twelve inches tall. But in Thundup's house there was no floor—only the ground itself. And there were no pillows or small tables. The only item of luxury was a lamp made of pewter, which burned yak butter. Thundup had kept this lamp burning for forty-nine days when Dolma, his wife, died. Better Tibetan homes would have had hand looms for weaving cloth. Thundup could not afford one.

One of the four rooms in Thundup's house was a kitchen. It had a hole in the roof under which a fireplace made of stone was located. That hole and the door gave the only light, for the house had no windows. Phuti had a bedroom for herself, and her father and brother shared a room. The beds were skins laid on the ground and covered with blankets. Winter was coming fast and Phuti knew that it would soon be so cold that she would probably have to sleep in her clothes to keep warm.

Thundup's and Jigmet's bedroom opened onto a fourth room that had an outside entrance. This was a storehouse with a stall for the *dzo*, the only work animal on Thundup's small farm. A cross between a cow and a yak, the *dzo* furnished the family with milk, cheese, and butter made in a wooden churn about three feet high. The *dzo* also furnished them with dung for cooking. The valley was treeless except for plantings of willow, poplar, and the common sea buckthorn—a silver-barked shrub with sharp spines and orange-yellow berries. Some of this wood was used for fuel. But the family preferred *dzo* dung, since it burned with a hot blue flame and made little smoke.

After the supplies had been stored and the animals watered and put in their pens, Jigmet prepared supper. He started a fire of dung, got it going well with a bellows, and put on a kettle for *gur gur cha*. They were going to have goat cheese, turnips from the garden, and mutton.

In theory Buddhists are not supposed to eat meat. In practice they do. The average Tibetan is greatly dependent on yak meat for his diet. The Buddhist, however, usually does not slaughter the animal. Each village or town of any size has a butcher who does the job for a fee. The butcher is usually a Mohammedan or a Chinese. In Phuti's village the butcher was a Chinese who was also a Mohammedan. Jigmet had four ewes in addition to the sheep that Thundup took on the trek. Shortly before Thundup's return the local butcher had slaughtered two of them. Jigmet had sold part of one. What was left hung in the corner of the storehouse.

It was the best meal Phuti had eaten since she and her father left on their long trek. They were a happy family as they sat around the small fireplace. There were dozens of questions to ask and much to tell. All could not be told that night, for Phuti could not long keep her eyes open. She was soon deep in her bed-roll, going quickly to sleep with one of the songs of Murli Dhar on her lips.

14

JIGMET CHOOSES
A WIFE

In the Moslem world, one man is entitled to four wives. This marriage practice is called polygamy. It was also long the custom in the Hindu world. But in Tibet and some of the regions of the Himalaya, a different kind of plural marriage is customary. It is called polyandry—a marriage where one woman has several husbands.

Phuti was the daughter of a polyandric marriage.

She remembered her mother, Dolma, very well. Her eyes were so bright, her nose and forehead so well shaped, her dark-yellow skin so clear and smooth that Phuti thought her the most beautiful woman in all the world. She had died of some strange disease when Phuti was ten years old. There were no doctors in the village, no hospital, no first-aid center, no medicine. There was a doctor in the monastery overlooking the village. But he was a doctor for the lamas only. Thundup tried to get him to attend Dolma when she was first taken ill, but he was too busy to leave the monastery. Thundup begged for days, and the doctor finally came. But by then Dolma was sinking fast.

Dolma was the daughter of a farmer. In Tibet it is customary for a girl who marries to become the wife not only of her husband but of all his brothers, too. Thundup had a younger brother Sonam. So when Dolma and Thundup were married Dolma had two husbands. But she wanted only Thundup. One night the three of them talked it over, with the result that Sonam left to become a lama in the monastery on the hill.

The memory of this episode came back to Thundup while he and Jigmet sat talking. Jigmet told Thundup that he planned to marry a village girl by the name of

Diki. Thundup knew her well and liked her. He also knew that by village custom the daughter-in-law could be his wife as well. The same would happen if Thundup married again. The stepmother would be Jigmet's wife, too.

As they talked, Thundup combed and braided his hair. This was a long, laborious ritual he performed twice a day. He combed his hair over his face and then worked out all the snarls. After the hair was smooth and straight, he parted it down the center and made two braids. Some Tibetan men work bright-colored cotton cloth into the braids. But Thundup did not bother with that. His braids were plain and tightly woven. He wound them on the top of his head and fastened them with hairpins, taking almost an hour for the ceremony.

After Jigmet broke the news of Diki to Thundup, the old man sat in silence, braiding his hair. When at last he wound the braids on his head, he turned to Jigmet and said, "Diki will be your wife alone." Thundup still remembered the anguish he had suffered when Sonam, his brother, claimed Dolma as a wife.

15

A LAMA LANDLORD

Each monastery has two departments—one devoted to religion, the other devoted to business. The spiritual work is headed by one lama; the business, by another. The business department is a large and active one. The monastery usually owns most of the land in the surrounding area and leases it to the farmers. The rental varies. Sometimes it is cash; usually it amounts to fifty percent of the crop.

The lama who is in charge of the business department of the monastery must draw the leases and confer with the tenant about the crops to be raised. He also supervises the harvest so that the monastery will get the landlord's share. He is a busy man, especially in the spring and fall. There are great demands on his time in the winter, too. Often a farmer runs out of food. Then the business lama must arrange a loan of food to be repaid at the next harvest. The lamas make sure that no farmer dies from starvation, but the monastery charges interest for its loans. A farmer who borrows twenty measures of grain from the monastery in February usually agrees to repay the monastery twenty-five measures in September. That is twenty-five percent interest for six months or at the rate of fifty percent a year.

Sometimes crops are scarce and large loans from the monastery are necessary. Sometimes the farmer is so deeply in debt to the monastery that he never can repay the loans. In that case the monastery usually forgives the debts.

The morning after Thundup and Phuti returned home the business lama appeared at their farm dressed in brownish red robes and riding a pure-white horse. Thundup went out to greet him, bowing low.

Then he and Thundup sat on a low stone wall and talked.

Thundup had much to tell the lama about the long journey. He told him how many rupees he had brought back, the number of sheep, the articles he had bartered for wool and salt. The lama went to the corral to see the sheep and suggested that Phuti drive them and Tashi to the red monastery on the hill. Thundup and Jigmet would load the other articles on the pony and the mule and bring them up.

It took all morning to transfer the goods to the monastery. A great mastiff, chained his whole lifetime near the warehouse and trained to be vicious, barked ferociously the entire time. When the last load was deposited on the warehouse platform, Thundup went to the office of the business lama.

The office was off the main courtyard of the monastery, which one could reach only by climbing a steep set of flagstone steps. Along the right-hand side of the stairway extended a series of drums that were constantly revolved clockwise by a running stream of water. Inside the drums were countless prayers written on parchment. As the drums revolved, these prayers were said for every visitor.

At the top of the steps was a large square courtyard with two-storied buildings on each side. These were sleeping, living, and eating quarters for the lamas. Here were classrooms where the lamas studied religion, philosophy, astronomy, and mathematics. Here was a chapel containing a statue of Buddha which was twice as large as a man. Here was a library filled with books. Here, too, were the offices of the lamas.

Thundup turned to his left as he entered the courtyard, almost falling over an old, old lady who constantly turned a large drum set in a frame. Inside the drum were thousands of prayers. The old lady was chanting *Om Mani Padme Hoom* as Thundup entered, and she did not stop as she held up one scrawny hand to ask for alms. Next to her was the most miserable looking man Thundup had ever seen. Thundup knew poverty and squalor, for he barely made a living each year. But the misery of this man was beyond anything he had known. His clothes were in rags, having been patched so often they were falling apart. He and the woman were not villagers but itinerant mendicants. Thundup was too poor to give to beggars. Yet he reached for a copper in his pocket and put it in the outstretched hand.

He crossed the courtyard and entered the center

door on the left. Here he was greeted by a young
lama. Every man who works or lives in a monastery is
a lama, but not many of the 500 in this monastery
were full-fledged lamas. Many were mere servants like
the young lama at the door, and servants they would
remain all their lives. They merely served the Incarnate One who was the monastery's head.

Thundup, cap in hand, went with the young lama
to the office of the chief business lama. It was a dark
room with one small window. Near the window was a
small, low table where the lama worked. It was
covered with papers, pens, and an inkwell. Along one
wall were large square cushions on which the lama sat
for meditation or for conferences. Another side of the
room had shelves filled with Tibetan books, which are
made up of long and narrow pages. The print is hand-
stamped. The pages are not bound but wrapped together in a piece of cloth, and the cloth is placed between two wooden boards held together with string.
On the wall across from the books was a miniature
shrine with a small statue of Buddha.

The lama was at his desk when Thundup was announced. Thundup stood while the lama went over
the accounts of the trip to Patseo. It seemed an eter-
nity before the lama spoke. When he did, he clapped

his hand for the attendant and ordered tea. Then he motioned Thundup to sit on the cushions.

Thundup had done well, exceptionally well. The corn he had purchased was superior. He had bought sandals, lanterns, kerosene, and cloth at a good price. He had received more for the sheep than had been expected. And the lama was particularly happy at the purchase of the six cans of snuff. The snuff alone was worth a small fortune, he said. Thundup interrupted to say that, if the snuff was sold at a good price, perhaps the lama could arrange for Phuti to have the prayer wheel she wanted. The lama not only promised that; he also promised Thundup the largest reward he had ever received for a trip to Patseo—300 rupees ($60.00).

Thundup was so happy over his good fortune that, as he came out of the dark room into the bright sunshine of the courtyard, he almost stumbled over five lamas sitting in a row and reciting the scriptures in unison.

16

THE DEMON TRAP

Thundup, Phuti, and Jigmet went to the monastery the next day to pray to the Buddha and give thanks. Phuti and Jigmet were barefoot, and Thundup left his sandals at the entrance to the temple. They stood inside the threshold for a few moments getting their eyes adjusted to the dark room. In the back of the temple on each side of the door was a tub of yak butter in which a wick was burning feebly. Each tub held several hundred pounds of butter and had been presented by a rich merchant. The tubs were lighted at the beginning of the new year and burned for twelve months.

Several rows of cushions were on each side of the center aisle. The left-hand section was filled with red-robed lamas whose shaved heads were bent as they chanted prayers in unison. At the end of each row stood a lama with a trumpet in his hand. Up front a high-ranking lama led the chant.

The walls of the temple were hung with paintings of figures with ferocious faces. They represented good spirits scowling at the evil ones. The seated Buddha, fully twelve feet high, was in the rear center of the temple. His arms were folded and he had the most serene face Phuti could imagine.

On each side of the Buddha were several statues of famous lamas who were identified with this monastery. In front of the Buddha were a dozen bowls holding water, barley, rice, and butter as offerings. Thundup brought barley and butter as his offering. In the Buddhist world women may not approach the Buddha and touch his feet. That may be done only by men. So Phuti had to stay behind the line marked for women. She prostrated herself there and said prayers for Thundup, for Jigmet, and for Murli Dhar.

Thundup and Jigmet approached the Buddha, touching his feet with their hands and placing their offerings in the bowls. Then they prayed. Their prayers were barely finished when the lamas with the trumpets filled the temple with a din that almost broke Phuti's eardrums.

As the family left the temple, they met a pilgrim who told them he had come 100 miles to pray at the monastery. He had made a prostration pilgrimage, measuring the entire distance with his body. This he accomplished by lying flat on his stomach with arms outstretched. Then he pulled himself up until his toes were on the mark made by his finger tips. Repeating this performance over and over again, he had taken three months to come the 100 miles. He wore knee pads and leather mittens for protection. He had chosen to make this prostration pilgrimage in order to do penance for his sins and gain merit.

On the way home Thundup announced that in honor of the family's safe return from Patseo he would place a new prayer flag on their home. He also announced that he would build a demon trap. He had heard of demon traps for years, and after talking with the lama at Patseo, he was convinced that one of these traps might have saved Dolma's life.

Using the lama's design, Thundup made a statue of clay two feet tall. Then he carved five sticks and fastened them into the clay at various angles. The sticks represented the three members of the family, Jigmet's new wife, and the spirit of Dolma. Next he wove colored thread from stick to stick until he had a rainbow-colored web that would catch any demon of sickness that might come by. The yellow, red, green, white, and blue threads represented earth, fire, water, air, and ether.

By placing a ball of wool at each corner, Thundup would eventually be able to tell whether any demons had been caught. When the balls of wool became damp, it would mean that the demons had been trapped. Then he would take the contraption to a cliff and throw it over, destroying the captured spirits.

17

GOOD VERSUS EVIL

There were many dances in Rudok during the fall and spring. One dance was done by women who formed a line, their arms around each other, and danced in a slow rhythm to the music of a drum and a horn. Phuti liked this dance best because she could take part.

The most exciting dance, however, was done by the men, who whirled and stomped so fast it was difficult to follow their movements. They would whirl in wide circles, then in smaller circles until they were spinning like tops. By that time they would be going so fast their faces became a blur. Dizziness never seemed to bother them.

Twice a year the monastery put on day-long dances in which the participants, mostly lamas, wore brilliant costumes and masks. The masks were carved out of wood and painted in bright colors. They represented spirits—some good, some bad. The bad spirits were Lust, Greed, Anger, Deceit, War. The masks worn by these spirits were hideous enough to scare a person. The forces of good were the stag and the yak. The dance portrayed the struggle between these two forces. Good always triumphed in the end, the stag and yak banishing the evil spirits. But the dance took all day to perform. And in between the serious scenes were dances by clowns, also wearing masks, who made the people laugh.

During the entire dance an orchestra of fifty or more pieces played. There were trumpets, hung with banners and tassels, that looked like clarinets. The drums stood on pedestals two feet high, and were struck by sticks bent into the shape of huge question marks. Attached to the drums were large cymbals.

Two horns twelve feet long played in unison. Their pitch was so deep it sounded as if it came out of the bowels of the earth. The musicians wore dark red robes and tall red hats. They played all day long with only an hour out for lunch.

The dance was presided over by two lamas—one a young boy of twelve called the Rinpoche or Incarnate One, the other called the Lobon. They sat on a low dais in the courtyard where the dance was held. The young boy wore dark red robes, a yellow shawl, and a peaked red hat that had no brim. The Lobon, also dressed in red and yellow, sat on the right of the boy. His hat was red with a great wide brim that flared up all around. The boy had in front of him a golden bell (*dilbu*) that he rang occasionally. Next to the bell was a gold thunderbolt (*dorje*) about six inches long, slightly bulging in the middle. Next to the thunderbolt was a feather duster in a holder that the boy waved now and then as part of the ritual.

This twelve-year-old boy was the head of the monastery. The last Rinpoche had died fourteen years ago. His soul had wandered for a while and then possessed the body of the present Rinpoche shortly after he was born. The lamas had found this boy by consulting an oracle who told them what village to visit and the kind of family to seek. Their search did not take long. They found the boy after a few weeks. They were sure he was the right one because he had the same scars as the deceased—a mark on the wrist and a mole on the back of the neck.

.When he was discovered he was brought at once to the monastery and educated by the Lobon. He had just turned twelve. Next summer he would go to Lhasa for eight years and complete his education. When he was twenty-one years old, he would return to Rudok and take full charge of his monastery.

All the villagers turned out for this dance. For this would be the last time they would see the Rinpoche for some years. They worshiped the lad. He was not only bright, he was also friendly and gay, smiling at all the people. Phuti had worked her way close to the dais where the Rinpoche and the Lobon sat. She could plainly hear the tinkle of the little gold bell and the shrill boyish voice of the Rinpoche as he chanted endlessly *Om Mani Padme Hoom.*

18

THE TURQUOISE
CARAVAN

It came to pass that Phuti did not return to Patseo the next summer. The lamas had other plans for Thundup. They wanted him to go to Lhasa with them. The Rinpoche was ready to enter the schools at Lhasa to complete his training. A large caravan of yaks and horses would be made up in June and take the summer to go to Lhasa and return. Thundup would go along to help the lamas in case any trading opportunities developed. The lama in charge of the business department mentioned to Thundup that he hoped to get a good buy of turquoises. If he did, he might want to send Thundup with a caravan down to Gangtok and Darjeeling to trade the gems for some of the wonderful Sikkim rice and for aluminum pots, pans, and plates.

Twenty people made up the group that left for Lhasa in June. A half-dozen horses were in the caravan and there were eighteen yaks loaded with food and baggage. The Rinpoche was carried in a chair, or palanquin, set on a platform which four men placed on their shoulders. The platform was covered with a panoply of yellow silk to protect the lad.

In case the Rinpoche wanted to ride, a pure-white Tibetan pony had been provided. In case he wanted to walk, there was a pure-white silk umbrella to hold over his head.

It would be a slow procession, for the Rinpoche would stop in many villages for ceremonies and visit at monasteries along the way.

Even in open country slow progress would be made. Yaks, which are huge animals of the ox family, are slow-walking. They groan as they walk and seldom go at a speed greater than one and a half miles an hour.

They carry great loads—three hundred pounds or more—and are sure-footed in rough terrain. They would die in the low valleys of India. They thrive only at high altitudes.

The journey seemed endless to Phuti, for there was nothing much that a girl could do. She helped around the fires at night and during the day she beat the yaks with a switch to make them go faster. But time passed very slowly.

One night they camped near a fresh-water lake called Yamdrok Tso. Many caravans were there. Dozens of fires glowed on the campgrounds.

Some of the caravans moved on at dawn. A half-dozen, including the Rinpoche's caravan, remained for a few days. This was an excellent camp, for a cold stream ran close by. It was a tributary of Yamdrok Tso. Though the lake is filled with brown trout, few people ever fish it. The lamas teach that it is not proper to take life of any form. Though yaks and sheep are butchered, the sin is not so great because the meat is divided up among a lot of people. But the whole of the sin would be on the head of the man who ate a trout. The taboo on fish is a severe one. Fish, like pork, are said to contain evil forces that will make men sick. Phuti saw hundreds of brown trout swimming out of the lake and up the stream to spawn. They were so thick she could easily have lifted them out by hand.

The delay at Yamdrok Tso was due to the desire of the Rinpoche and the Lobon to visit a nearby monastery presided over by a woman. She is one of the holiest women in Tibet and is supposed to have unusual powers. It is said that she can turn herself into a sow. In fact, she is called the Thunderbolt Sow. Once when a Chinese army threatened the monastery, she is supposed to have turned all the lamas into pigs. When the Chinese soldiers saw this happening, they were filled with terror and fled.

The delay at Yamdrok Tso brought a good reward. On the third day a mailman came through from Lhasa. He traveled on foot, running most of the time, with the mail bag on his back and a spear in his hand. His section of the trail was about ten miles long. He had received the bag from one courier and would pass it on to another. Thus the mail would be carried to India in relays by dozens of runners. The mailman talked to the lamas and told them that a caravan of turquoise was on its way from Lhasa.

When the turquoise caravan reached Yamdrok Tso, the lamas had long negotiations with the Tibetan traders. Finally a bargain was made, and Thundup and Phuti turned south to India with their precious cargo and a dozen horses. Thundup had instructions from the lamas to go to Gangtok, capital of Sikkim. He was to stay there all winter, since the high passes would probably close with snow before he could make the return trip. He would come back to western Tibet in early summer.

There are three high passes to cross on the way to Gangtok. Thundup and Phuti had not gone far before they crossed Karo La, nearly 17,000 feet high. In four more days they came to Gyantse. So far they were backtracking. From Gyantse on, they would travel south through unfamiliar land.

They made many detours to find good grazing for the horses. But each day Thundup and Phuti were on the move by dawn. In less than a week they came to Tang La Pass, which is 15,000 feet high, crossed it, and dropped down to a 14,000-foot plain. It was a clear day and the Himalayan peaks stood in glory. Chomolhari (23,996 feet) rose nearly two miles above the plain and seemed so close one could touch it.

The winds are fierce on this plain—so fierce that some caravans do not travel during midday. But Thundup and Phuti never stopped except to visit with yak herders in their black wool tents. And they were usually rewarded by a cup of *gur gur cha* (called *so za* in eastern Tibet).

They were on this cold and windy plain for about a week. And during that time they met several caravans heading north from India. Some were made up of yaks, some of horses, and some of men who themselves were the beasts of burden. Some men carried beds in crates on their backs; others carried large chairs; some bore tables. But the strangest sight of all was that of men carrying jeeps on their backs. The jeeps, which were American made, had been bought by Indian traders and driven to Gangtok. There they were taken apart and made up into small parcels. Then the parcels were put in slings and carried by coolies 300 miles to Lhasa. They were destined for Red China.

Thundup talked to the man who was in charge of this caravan and who rode a horse behind the coolies who carried the jeeps. There were six jeeps in the caravan, and he charged as freight 1,800 rupees ($360.00) to bring each one over the Himalaya on the backs of his coolies.

Thundup and Phuti soon dropped off the high Tibetan plateau and descended through forests of pine, fir, and spruce to Tibet's frontier town, Yatung. In another day they climbed to Nathu-La Pass (14,-800 ft.)—the divide between Tibet and India—and then dropped down and down into a hot and uncomfortable valley. They first came to the slopes where the rhododendron grows. In the Himalaya the rhododendron is a tree, not a bush, and grows thirty feet or more high. It furnishes the best wood for cooking to be found on the southern slopes of the Himalaya. There were also huge strawberries along the trail, a dark-purple iris, yellow and red poppies by the acre, cinquefoil, and other flowers almost too numerous to catalogue.

Thundup and Phuti came down to Gangtok in a driving rain which shut out all the scenic views of the high peaks. The lower they went the thicker grew the forests. There were many birds familiar to the West along these southern slopes—kingfishers, magpies, flycatchers, finches, thrushes. And even the magpie was gaily colored. Moss and lichens covered the trees. Masses of white orchids hung down from the boughs. Ferns stood twelve feet high. Underbrush was so thick one could see only a few feet into the forest. A few monkeys crossed the trail. A great shiny snake ran underfoot, scaring the horses. Soon the caravan was in a bamboo forest that was dense and suffocating. This section of the Himalaya gets over 200 inches of rain a year. Most of it falls in the summer months when the monsoons come up from the ocean.

The dampness was bad enough. But what made the trip thoroughly uncomfortable were the leeches. These are small bloodsuckers about an inch long and thinner than a match. They seem to sense the presence of a caravan, for they descend on everyone with a vengeance. They race along the ground, drop off overhanging branches, or catch on clothing or skin as one brushes the undergrowth. They fasten themselves into the nostrils of the horses until the animals can hardly breathe. They dig into a person's skin and suck his blood.

Those accustomed to Himalayan travel protect themselves from leeches by putting tobacco leaves around their ankles or by bathing their legs in salt water. But Thundup and Phuti came unprepared. Phuti was barefoot and Thundup had only sandals. By the time they reached the large caravansery at Gangtok their legs were bleeding badly from the leech bites, and the noses of all the horses were swollen.

19

ABOMINABLE SNOWMEN

Thundup and Phuti spent the winter in Gangtok and Darjeeling. Thundup was a patient trader and finally sold the turquoise for a good price. He bought in exchange choice Sikkim rice, hardware and utensils, silver boxes made in the neighboring principality of Bhutan, and a supply of cardamon—the spice which is as famous in Sikkim as the sweet Sikkimese oranges.

During the winter Thundup and Phuti learned

much of the folklore of the mountains. They learned, for example, about the abominable snow man, which is said to live in the high Himalaya. Some doubt its existence. But the people of Sikkim believe there is such an animal. When I was in Sikkim, I visited with the Maharaja—a short, slight, soft-spoken man and a devout Buddhist. He told me that he believes the abominable snow man exists—that one night at Gangtok he looked out the window and saw one racing across his lawn.

Many hillmen believe that any abominable snow man will kill them. The hillmen call it the *yeti*. It is supposed to be of either the bear or ape family—grayish with a pointed head and about four or five feet tall. Tenzing, the famous Sherpa, told me that he believes the *yeti* exists and that it is an ape. Britishers have photographed an apelike footprint with five toes made by some unknown animal in the high snow. And Japanese expeditions to the Himalaya have brought confirmatory evidence that the *yeti* actually exists. Though many hillmen insist they have seen the *yeti*, there has as yet been no scientific confirmation of its existence.

There are also legends about a mysterious snow woman. She is said to have only one leg, and she always carries a pipe between her lips. She frequents the high snow fields and whistles at passers-by. Her whistle is thought to entice men onto the glaciers, where she devours some and makes love to others.

Most Himalayan peaks are surrounded with legends and superstitions. It is said that there is a chair of gold on top of Everest. According to the story there was great religious activity in Tibet in the eighth century A.D. Buddhist lamas came from India to spread their faith there. The King of Tibet preferred Buddhism over other religions. He declared he would make it the official religion of Tibet if the Buddhist lamas won a contest—a race to the top of Everest. The contenders were Hoshang Mahayan of China and Kamalashila of India. Kamalashila waited until Hoshang Mahayan had nearly reached the top. Then Kamalashila lifted himself by sheer spiritual power through the thin air. He was sitting on the peak in the chair of gold when his Chinese competitor arrived.

In 1952 and 1954 the Japanese brought expeditions to the Himalaya in an attempt to climb Manaslu (26,657 feet). They failed in the attempt but incurred the wrath of the hill people. To the hill people Manaslu is a sacred mountain and they believed that the Japanese, by attempting to climb it, had angered the gods. After the Japanese left, an avalanche destroyed an ancient monastery and killed several lamas. Then came a drought, injuring the crops. On top of that came a smallpox epidemic. When the Japanese returned in 1956, they were met by an aroused populace who refused them passage to Manaslu.

But the Japanese leader Yuko Maki was a devout Buddhist. He presented money to help rebuild the monastery, Buddhist books for the library, and smallpox vaccine for the people. He then convinced the local authorities that his climb up Manaslu would be a Buddhist pilgrimage to a holy place. With that assurance the Japanese expedition was cleared. The alpinists made their last camp at a height of 23,622 feet. A Japanese by the name of Imainishi and a Sherpa named Gyalzen conquered Manaslu on May 9, 1956, in a six-hour climb with the aid of oxygen equipment. They stayed on top an hour; and in fulfillment of their leader's promise, they offered Buddhist prayers there. Two days later another team from the same expedition also reached the top. Actually, the top of Manaslu consists of four sharp pinnacles, the highest of which is only wide enough for one person to stand upon.

Kangchenjunga means "The Great Snow with the

Five Treasures," which refers to the five separate peaks on the mountain. The five treasures are (1) salt, (2) gold and turquoise, (3) holy books and wealth, (4) weapons, (5) crops and medicine. There are many legends about Kangchenjunga.

It is believed that the top of Kangchenjunga is the home of spirits who would be angry if anyone set foot on its top. Kangchenjunga was finally climbed May 25, 1955, by George Band and Joe Brown, members of a British team headed by Charles Evans. (Band and Brown used oxygen equipment.) Another team, Norman Hardie and Tony Streather, went up the next day. Before the assault they were entreated by the Buddhist priests or lamas of Sikkim not to step on the top—to keep it sacred and undisturbed. Evans promised to respect their wish. Though conquering Kangchenjunga, the British climbers stopped twenty feet short of the actual summit and about five feet below it.

Kangchenjunga has been deified. The Sikkimese call it the god Kuvera, who is represented as being red in color, armed, and mounted on a white mountain lion. He is called the war god, and to appease him the people put on dances.

The most famous is the war dance. Lamas and

young men are dressed as warriors with swords, shields, heavy garments, and grotesque colored masks carved from wood. The dance is a strenuous one, showing great skill in the use of the sword. The theme of the dance is a plea to Kuvera to protect the faith of the church and the security of the nation and to bring peace and prosperity to the people. The followers of Kuvera fight the enemies of the god and defeat them.

Thundup and Phuti saw this dance in the full moon of the seventh Tibetan month (which is August) just after they had crossed the high Himalayan passes from Tibet.

20

A HIMALAYAN WEDDING

Phuti and Murli Dhar met again at Patseo the following summer. They had been together only a few days when they decided to marry. Murli Dhar spoke to Thundup about it, and he was agreeable. So plans were made to have a Hindu priest perform the ceremony in the Kulu Valley.

When Thundup had made all his bargains and the father of Murli Dhar had wound up his affairs at

Patseo, the four started south to Kulu. They took turns riding the three horses in the small caravan. It was a clear bright day when they crossed Rothang Pass and started down the easy trail laid with slate slabs leading to Kulu. The weather was so good that they reached Kulu in four days.

Murli Dhar arranged for Thundup and Phuti to have a separate cottage of their own. Then plans for the wedding were arranged. A Hindu priest was consulted about the day and hour of the wedding. The priest, who was very old and thin with a silky stubble of a beard, asked the date of birth of Phuti and Murli Dhar and said he would consult an astrologist. A propitious day and a propitious hour would have to be selected. Only an astrologist would know when the planets under which Phuti and Murli Dhar were born would be in the most harmonious relationship.

The next day the priest announced that August 7th would be the day of the wedding and 11:00 P.M. the hour.

The village buzzed with excitement over this wedding of an Indian boy and a Tibetan girl. The parents and relatives of Murli Dhar prepared food for feasts and rituals. There were dances at night and many fireworks. Gifts were sent to Murli Dhar by Thundup and to Phuti by the parents of Murli Dhar. The father of Murli Dhar sent a man to measure Phuti for her wedding dress. The day before the wedding Murli Dhar and Phuti were presented with the sacred colored thread called the *kangna,* which was tied around their wrists.

On the wedding day Murli Dhar sent Phuti a mirror, a comb, perfume, saffron, jewels, and a shawl. These were symbolic gifts, indicating that in the future Phuti would adorn herself only with the things her husband provided.

The wedding was performed in the courtyard of Murli Dhar's home. The priest made a fire and poured butter on it to make it burn brightly. Thundup gave Phuti's hand to Murli Dhar, who prayed that he and Phuti would always be faithful to each other. Then he and Phuti walked around the nuptial fire together. Murli Dhar sprinkled holy water on Phuti from a bowl held by the priest and prayed that her eyes, heart, and mind would be his always and that his would be hers. Then the assembled group recited prayers in unison asking the one Universal Spirit to bless the married pair.

Thundup left for Tibet the next morning on one of the horses. Murli Dhar and Phuti would follow in two days and catch up with him. Murli Dhar had decided to be a trader on the great caravan route. He and Phuti would spend their first winter in Rudok.

The two days following the wedding were days of merriment. A severe storm broke with much rain, lightning, and thunder. But it did not interfere with the feasting and dancing. The third day was bright and clear. Murli Dhar and Phuti left early, riding horseback up the trail heading north. They pushed hard to cross Rothang Pass before dark.

They had left the pine and chestnut forests and reached green open slopes when they saw many dead horses and cattle by the trail. The rain storm in the Kulu Valley had turned to a blizzard at Rothang Pass, and the livestock had perished in it. The vultures circling overhead had already eaten out the eyes of the dead animals. Murli Dhar and Phuti shuddered at the sight and became worried over Phuti's father.

When they arrived at Patseo, the couple found that tragedy had indeed stalked Thundup. He had caught a severe cold in the dreadful blizzard. There are no doctors in the Himalaya. Lacking medical care,

Thundup died of pneumonia shortly after Murli Dhar and Phuti joined him at Patseo.

When at last they took the trail leading north to Tibet, the young couple walked with heavy hearts.

EPILOGUE

The Himalaya—once a great barricade against the invaders from the north—no longer provides the south with real protection. Of course today, as always, snow and ice block the trails for most of the year. Phuti, Murli Dhar and all the other mountain people to the north can pass over the high mountain barrier only during three months of each year. But the airplane has worked a vast change. Russia and China—

aggressive communist countries—occupy the country to the north of the Himalaya, and they have dotted it with air bases. Every city to the south is now within easy bombing range winter and summer.

The communist threat is not entirely military. The aim of Russia and China is to win the hearts and the minds of these mountain people to the communist cause. People like Phuti and Murli Dhar live in great poverty. There are few schools for their children. Doctors, medical care, dentists, and hospitals are practically nonexistent. There is little opportunity for man or child to improve his lot. Generation after generation of mountain people seem destined to misery.

The Communists exploit this situation, using propaganda to stir discontent and revolt among the masses. The defenses against this type of communist penetration are twofold. The Moslem and Buddhist churches are telling the people not to be misled by communist promises. The liberal progressive governments of India and Pakistan are introducing reform measures to alleviate the misery of the border people.

Meanwhile, the Himalaya, with their ever changing colors and towering majesty, top the scene. Although man has succeeded in conquering the highest of them, they still have about them, and always will, an air of mystery, of foreboding. "Pass at your risk," they seem to say to the traveler, to the invader. The simple and the wise alike understand the warning.

INDEX

Index